From the Holocaust to a New Dawn

David Shachar

Copyright © David Shachar
Jerusalem 2011/5771

All rights reserved. No part of this publication may be translated, reproduced, stored in a retrieval system or transmitted, in any form or by any means, electronic, mechanical, photocopying, recording or otherwise, without express written permission from the publishers.

This book was published with the support of
The Azrieli Foundation

Cover Design and Typesetting by S. Kim Glassman

ISBN: 978-965-229-546-0

1 3 5 7 9 8 6 4 2

Gefen Publishing House, Ltd.	Gefen Books
6 Hatzvi Street	11 Edison Place
Jerusalem 94386, Israel	Springfield, NJ 07081, USA
972-2-538-0247	1-800-477-5257
orders@gefenpublishing.com	orders@gefenpublishing.com

www.gefenpublishing.com

Printed in Israel   *Send for our free catalogue*

Approbation by Knesset Member Ephraim Sneh

July 19, 2006

What is the history of a people? It is the accumulation of millions of personal biographies. It is possible to understand the history of a people through the fate of its members.

Such is the story of the life of David Shachar, which can be summed up with the clichéd term "From the Holocaust to Rebirth."

This autobiography represents the course that the Jewish people has traversed in the last sixty years of the twentieth century.

The events of the Holocaust and the survivors' difficult journey of survival, the illegal immigration to Israel, the fighting of the War of Independence, the building of the development towns, the harnessing and mobilizing of Jews to the development of a unique military technology – these are the stations in the life of David Shachar, and these are the great deeds of the entire generation of the people and the state.

David Shachar wrote in humility one of the wonderful stories of a man of initiative, of a pioneering and volunteering spirit. It is important that this book has been published; it is important that it be read by the youth in order that they know with what suffering this state was established, and how hard it was to maintain it in the early years. It is because of people like David Shachar that it exists to this day.

Ephraim Sneh
Knesset Member
Chairman of the Avodah Faction

Approbation by Ephraim Kaye

David Shachar wrote his autobiography called "From the Holocaust to a New Dawn" that takes the reader from his birth in the small Polish town of Krasnosielc in 1930 through his experiences during World War II, his emigration to the Land of Israel and his life over the past sixty years in the State of Israel.

This book is unique, as is every story written by every survivor. Having said that, David has written a story that encompasses not only the personal tragedy of his immediate family but what he did "with his Holocaust" during the past sixty years here in the State of Israel. The story of his "rebirth" is one of unprecedented creativity, courage and self-sacrifice that is the essence of Israel today. His story stands as a shining example of what one person can do to make a difference.

David Shachar is a role model for us all.

Ephraim Kaye
Director, International Seminars for Educators
The International School for Holocaust Studies
Yad Vashem

Approbation by Arieh Lova Eliav

An Appreciation

The memories of David Shachar are like a journey through the tunnel of time: from wanderings in Poland to the life of a refugee in World War II, and on to a soldier's life fighting the Nazis.

After a period of studies in electronics, David made *aliya* to Israel. He volunteered immediately for the Palmach and fought in its ranks in the War of Independence.

A few years after the founding of the State of Israel, David went with his family to live in Kiryat Shmona. He worked incessantly to advance the developing city, using his qualifications and abilities to develop technology in the border area.

Many years afterwards, David Shachar served as a senior representative of the Israel Aircraft Industries with the Ministry of Defense in Europe and Israel and did much to develop and advance Israel's defense industry.

David never lost sight of his memories of World War II, and he devoted himself to memorializing the bravery of the 30,000 Jewish soldiers who fell in the Polish armies. With his blessed initiative, the outstanding monument in their memory was established at the military cemetery on Mount Herzl in Jerusalem.

And thus, through tragedy and war and a desire for peace, through building industry and volunteering in development areas, the varied life of David Shachar and the Jewish and Zionist missions in which he operated serve as a model for our generation and for our times.

Arieh Lova Eliav
Former Knesset member
one of the founders of the Labor party and recipient of the Israel Prize

Dedication

I dedicate this book to my friend Sami Shamoon, who passed away on May 29, 2009. Sami, a noble soul, helped me very much, together with Yossi Maimon of the Merhav Company and the Soldiers' Memorial Department of the Ministry of Defense, in the establishment of the memorial to the fifty thousand officers and soldiers who fell in World War II in the service of the Polish armies on the various fronts, including the hundreds of officers, prisoners of war, who were murdered in the Katyn forests in 1940. Sami Shamoon also came to my aid in various memorializing and documentation activities and made a significant contribution to the fund for establishing a Jewish museum in Warsaw. It is proper that his sympathetic outlook regarding Jews of all backgrounds become an educational and moral message for present and future generations. May his memory be blessed.

This book is dedicated as well to the future generations of teachings and lessons that come to us from the past, as well as to the memory of my dear family: my father, Haim Himmelfarb, may God avenge his blood, horribly slaughtered by Nazis together with sixty other notables of Krasnosielc on September 5, 1939, the fifth day of war; my mother, Hinda Rivka Kuropatwa Himmelfarb who after my father's death guided the family along their difficult path until their arrival in Israel in 1948, where she died in 1981; my older brother Yosef, who, "ascending" to Israel as a pioneer in 1935, acted as a representative of Poalei

Agudat Israel in the rescue of surviving European exiles, and died in Jerusalem in 1984; my brother Moshe, who died in 1943 from cold and starvation in the Soviet gulag of the Komi district, in northern Russia; and my brother Hershel, murdered by Nazis during the first days of their USSR invasion, in June 1941. In memory, also, of all my father's and mother's families who perished in the Shoah, most of them in the Treblinka extermination camp.

I dedicate this book also to my recently deceased brothers Yitshak and Elimelech, may their memory be blessed. Their brotherly love and affection contributed strongly to that feeling of family solidarity which was so important in helping me to meet and overcome the many difficulties I had to face throughout my life.

My deepest gratitude goes to my wife, Chaya, for her patience, encouragement and support during all these years spent researching and writing this book.

Contents

Chapter One
My Childhood in Krasnosielc, Poland 1

Chapter Two
The War Begins 13

Chapter Three
Survival in Siberia 29

Chapter Four
From Poland to Paris 53

Chapter Five
In the Palmach 67

Chapter Six
Acclimatization in Israel 83

Chapter Seven
From the City to the Border – Seven Years in Kiryat Shmona 93

Chapter Eight
Joining the Defense Industry 113

Chapter Nine
My First Assignment in Italy 119

Chapter Ten
Resuming Work at the Israel Aircraft Industries 133

Chapter Eleven
We Return to Italy – Representing Tahal 137

Chapter Twelve
Commemorating the Past 143

Chapter Thirteen
In Retirement 163

Appendix

Curriculum Vitae for David Shachar 167
The Murder of the Jews of Krasnosielc 169
Letter from Haim Himmelfarb 172
Letter from Yehoshua (Shaiki) Gavish,
    Chairman, Dor Hapalmach 174
The Projects of the Kiryat Shmona Development Company 175
Letter from the Ministry of Defense 177
Letter from Mordecai Peltzur 178
Plaque to Mr. Sami Shamoon 180
My Town – On the Krasnosielc Community 181
Recommendation for the President's Volunteer Citation 183
Letter from Captain Ephraim Talmon 184
Letter from the Skvirsky Family 185
Impressions, Experiences and Lessons
    on "Operation Krasnosielc" 187

CHAPTER ONE

My Childhood in Krasnosielc, Poland

One sunny September morning in the town of Krasnosielc, Poland, a midwife was summoned to come immediately to the house of Hinda Himmelfarb, the wife of the *shohet* and *mohel* Haim Himmelfarb. The midwife arrived holding a big basin made of sheet metal. The children of the family were quickly moved out of the house and in no time the crying of a baby was heard within its walls.

"Congratulations," the midwife announced. "You have a son, another son."

Thus I was born, on Tuesday, September 16, 1930, the eighth child in the family. My father circumcised me and gave me the name David. In time another two children were added to the family.

My father, Haim Himmelfarb, was born in 1890 to his parents Avigdor and Mally Himmelfarb in Pokrzewnice in southeast Poland, on the banks of the Vistula River. His father was a successful businessman. My father had only one brother and three sisters: Yankel, Bruria, Esther and Sara. Except for Sara who immigrated in the 1920s to Argentina, the rest of my father's siblings remained in Poland.

In his youth my father studied in heder and when he became bar mitzvah he was sent to study at a yeshiva of the Gur Hasidim in Gora

Calwaria (Gur, in Yiddish). This city had the largest section of the Hasidic movement during that period.

My mother, Hinda-Rivka, was born in 1892 to Ephraim-Yitshak and Hanna (née Eisenberg) Kuropatwa (literally, "bird song"). Her father was born at Parczew. The family continued to live in Gniewoszow, a town in southeast Poland, where he served as a *shohet*.

My mother was the first child, followed by two sons and five more daughters: Shalom, Yosef, Miriam, Dinah, Mindel, Golda and Gita. When the girls grew to maturity, Grandfather Ephraim-Yitshak decided to marry them off to *shohatim*. From his personal experiences as a *shohet*, he knew that his work was considered an honorable trade although it did not pay a high wage. His sons Shalom and Yosef, however, chose different professions. Shalom was engaged in commerce and Yosef was a clerk in the town. Yosef was also the only one in the family who later became a religious Zionist. Once the daughters were married they went to live with their husbands in various places throughout Poland.

When my mother became of marriageable age, her parents looked for a match among the yeshiva students. Because of their relations with the rabbi of Gur, they were introduced to my father who was studying then at the Gur Yeshiva and was considered a Torah prodigy. The wedding took place in 1911. In keeping with the custom of the time, after the marriage my father went to live at my mother's house in Gniewoszow for a while. This period of time after the marriage was called "eating kest."

During this period my father learned to become a *shohet* from my grandfather and after the birth of his first son, Yosef, my father began to look for a position as a *shohet*.

In time ten children were born to my parents. The family consisted of seven sons (Yosef, Moshe, Hershel, Aharon, Yitshak, David and Elimelech) and three daughters (Bronia, Leah and Malka).

The growing family moved a few times while searching for a suitable position as a *shohet* but eventually settled in 1924 in the town of Krasnosielc.

The small town of Krasnosielc was located about sixty miles northeast of Warsaw and about twenty miles from the border with East Prussia. The location of the town, and especially its closeness to the German border, would be of great significance in determining the fate of the townspeople and of my family in the not-too-distant future.

The name of the town, Krasnosielc, originated with the Krasinski family, who founded the town in the seventeenth century as a Christian agricultural settlement. *Sielc* means "a settlement" in Polish and Krasno is taken from the name of the family. Jews began to settle in the town only in the second half of the eighteenth century. Since in the beginning there was only a small Jewish community of 250 people; its members belonged to synagogues in neighboring communities until it became an independent community itself. Only at the end of the nineteenth century was the synagogue built in the town. The synagogue knew both times of happiness and moments of terror; it is still in existence to this very day. Krasnosielc was placed on the map by the Hollywood Warner brothers. Their parents and one brother (Harry) were born there.

On the eve of World War II there were about two thousand Jews living in Krasnosielc, about half the population of the town. They lived mainly in the center of the town and were engaged in commercial activities and trades such as metalwork, carpentry and shoemaking and also businesses connected with community life and religion. The town had a rabbi, two *shohatim* and religious judges. The town had both rich and poor Jews and mutual help played a very important role in the community.

Most of the Jews in the town were Orthodox, and on weekdays they usually prayed in two shtieblach. One was for Gur and Amshinov Hasidim, and the other was for Radzymin Hasidim. Secular members of the community held the Jewish tradition in honor and on the Sabbath and holidays they prayed together with the Orthodox in the great synagogue at the center of the town. The town also boasted a big library and Hebrew school. At the Hebrew school the Jews of the town learned the Torah but it also served as a meeting place.

It was possible to meet a wide variety of political and philosophical opinions in Krasnosielc. There were members of Agudat Yisrael, Mizrachi, Hovevei Zion and the Bund. Even the Communist Party found fertile ground in the town because of the poor economic conditions of a part of the population. There were also the youth movements of Agudat Yisrael and Mizrachi, as well as Hashomer Hatzair and Betar.

My father had a number of functions in the town. He was the *shohet*, one of the two cantors in the town, a gabai, a shofar blower and a *mohel*, in which last function he circumsized all of his male children. He received a rather humble salary from the community for all these functions and in the religious hierarchy of the town he was considered second in importance to

Rabbi Yitshak Yosef Zilberberg. In addition to his work in Krasnosielc he often performed *shehitah* for Jews who lived in the neighboring villages. We didn't grow up in a rich family but we also didn't suffer from want.

My father devoted a great deal of his time to community matters, and was involved in all the challenges that befell the local Jewish community. In addition he spent much time learning Torah. In the morning he would go to prayers in the shtiebel and participate in Torah lessons which took place there in the afternoon. Often the rabbi and some of those learned in the Torah, my father among them, would gather to discuss various religious questions.

My father, a Gerrer Hasid, had become well aquainted with the Rebbe's court during his youth in the yeshiva and he shared his knowledge with other townspeople. Several times during the year – on the Sabbath of Hanukkah, on the Sabbath following Sukkot and on the Shavuot holiday – he would travel with the rabbi and some other Hasidim to the Rebbe of Gur's court. At the court they absorbed spiritual food, learning Torah and discussing various questions pertaining to Jewish law. Since I was among the youngest children in the house, I was never privileged to join them on the trip to the rabbi's court although my older brothers Yosef, Moshe and Aharon went with them often and from them I heard their impressions of those visits. One of the stories I heard from my father which I remember very well concerns a visit my father paid to the rabbi's court at the end of the first year of his marriage. The tish that my father wanted to witness was scheduled for noon, but Father knew that in order to find a good observation point he had to get there a few hours earlier. He arrived at the place at six in the morning. After a long wait, close to twelve o'clock, another Hasid arrived and demanded that my father give up his place. My father refused, so the other Hasid decided to climb on my father's shoulders. My father couldn't bear the Hasid's weight and fainted after a few minutes. And on that visit my father wasn't able to fulfill his dream of seeing the rabbi sitting at the head of the banquet table.

All his life my father maintained a connection with members of his family, especially by letter writing. Once in a while his parents sent him money. When my brother Aharon reached bar mitzvah age, he sent my grandfather a letter about a new interpretation of the Torah. In return my grandfather sent him twenty zloty – a sizable amount for those days.

Because of the distances and difficulty in traveling my father didn't visit them often. On special occasions such as family celebrations and during difficult times he put aside all his reasons for not going and went to visit. This happened when his sister Esther was married, when his father was sick and when his mother passed away.

My father was very concerned that we receive a religious education and obey all the commandments. He was hard and unbending in this matter and did not tolerate any deviations. He told us what behavior was permissible and what was forbidden. I was very careful to walk the straight line, and enjoyed my father's favor. But even as a child doubts and questions began to bother my conscience. These doubts increased as I got older but I kept them to myself.

I was always well behaved and given to compromise so that I received a lot of affection from those around me. My brothers complained that people liked me because of my looks. My sisters refused to go with me to the synagogue on the excuse that every step of the way people would stop us in order to pinch my cheeks. My mother derived great pleasure from her handsome boy and spit "Foo Foo" as a remedy against the evil eye lest it take away my good looks.

My mother did not have much of a formal education, but because of her innate intelligence she acquired for herself a sizeable amount of knowledge by reading. She was familiar with and knew how to quote from the Talmud and Midrash and could recount tales from the history of Judaism. In the absence of Jewish schools during the war years, she would tell us stories from the Bible, among them the story of David and Shaul and the story of the Exodus. She also told us about events from various periods of Jewish history: the First Temple, the Second Temple, the Diaspora in Babylon and the Inquisition in Spain. This spiritual food from my mother made things easier for us during the hard days that we later suffered and helped us to strengthen and deepen our Jewish identity.

Like most women in that period my mother was dedicated to the different kinds of work around the house and to the education of her children. She was outstanding in her energy and never wasted her time. I often saw her busy with house matters until the wee hours of the morning. On Thursday she was busy all night cooking for the Sabbath. She never permitted herself to be sick, and if we found her lying on her bed we knew that she was beginning to give birth and the midwife was on her way to the house. We children were pushed out of the house during these times and when we returned we were received by another brother or sister.

My mother was a strong woman, assertive and very involved in what was going on around her. She was careful in keeping the commandments and helping her neighbors and often sent my sisters to distribute food to the town's poor. Her high status in the town was due to being the wife of the *shohet* as well as due to her character and intelligence. Many women came to our house to get advice from her regarding money, matchmaking, health and the selection of a yeshiva for a maturing son. My parents knew about the various yeshivas and were therefore able to advise parents on the appropriate choice for their son. My parents also helped the community by adopting the popular custom of *essen tag* (eating days), according to which yeshiva boys ate their meals each day with a different family.

One of the outstanding characteristics of my mother was the ability to honor the opinion of others. When my brother Hershel distanced himself from religion and went in a political direction different from hers it caused her great pain but she didn't prevent him from doing it. When, in solidarity with the working class, he chose to work in a workshop sewing torn flour sacks, thereby endangering his health from excessive dust inhalation, my mother honored his decision this time also. She sent him a letter advising him to drink boiled milk every morning. The honor that Mother expressed toward our decisions as maturing youths and toward the road we chose as mature persons was a great help to me at various stages of my life and served to strengthen me through the years.

Relations of mutual respect and esteem existed between my father and mother. Father was grateful to Mother for the care she gave to all matters relating to the household and her concern for our education and development and for managing the household with the small salary he made. Mother, on her side, honored Father for his being a *talmid hakham*, a status that was held in high regard within the community. She helped him maintain his position and made sure that we had guests from the top of the religious hierarchy in the town. She felt superior to the townspeople but she always tried to elevate the community she had influence upon. She maintained a close relationship with her family by writing letters and visiting.

Our family lived in a one-story house. The house had a kitchen and four rooms: a living room, my parents' room and two rooms for the children. One room was for the boys and the other for the girls, and in addition there was a large porch with a glass enclosure. The porch served during the summer as an additional bedroom. In the back of the house was a wide yard with pear and apple trees.

Sanitary conditions during that period were far from perfect. We were not inoculated as it is done today and various diseases, especially diptheria and influenza, were common. When necessary we were treated by a Jewish doctor and often we were helped by folk remedies. One day when I had a bad fever my father made me suck on a piece of absorbent cotton soaked in wine from Eretz Yisrael. The adults thought that it had remedial powers. I liked the wine, and its sweet-sharp taste remains part of the treasured memories of my childhood.

Each day a maid would come to our house, a Christian who was one of the town residents. She helped my mother with the cleaning and bringing water from the pump in the town square. Mother preferred to cook herself, since she didn't trust a maid to observe the kashrut laws. My sisters helped mother now and again. As was the custom then, the girls in the family were mobilized for house chores and we the boys were exempted. This sometimes caused resentment on the part of my sisters. I volunteered now and again to help bring the water although I wasn't expected to because of my young age.

Most of the consumer products were bought at a few shops in the town, the majority of which were owned by Jews. We received new shoes and new clothes for the holidays, especially before Passover and Rosh Hashanah. My mother used to buy fruit and vegetables on market day, which took place in the town once a week. During this market the farmers from the villages in the vicinity sold their agricultural products to all the residents of the town. We always bought fresh vegetables and fruits which we stored in the cellar of our house. In the cellar also stood barrels in which we pickled cucumbers and cabbage during the winter. My father often received pieces of meat for his services as a *shohet*. On the eve of Yom Kippur he brought home chickens and we would grab them, swinging them over our head as kapparot.

Once every two months a big operation, "Laundry Day," took place and the house was a mess. Mother and her helpers worked very hard all day. First, they brought water from the well and heated it. After that, they washed and rubbed huge piles of laundry on a metal washboard, afterwards hanging them to dry in the yard.

There were many preparations for the Sabbath and all of us took part in them. On Thursday my mother began to cook and bake: noodles, challas, cakes, gefilte fish and the rest of the delicious foods that piled up in the kitchen. The smell of food filled the whole house. We were all used to taking a bath before the Sabbath. Mother and the older girls bathed at home. Father and my older brother went to the mikvah, while we the small ones bathed in a big tub (*pilla*) full of hot water. Mother supervised us and made sure that we remained clean and that not a speck of dirt got on the Sabbath clothes that we wore.

Before mother lit the Sabbath candles, each one of us placed some money for the Hachmei Lublin Yeshiva into a box that stood in our house. After that all of the family went to the large synagogue in the town center to welcome the Sabbath. When we returned we sat at the large table in the dining room and welcomed the Sabbath, singing *Shalom Aleikhem* and reciting the blessing over the wine. Father blessed the two large challas and for the sake of a feeling of independence he blessed each of the children on their own small challas. The festive Sabbath meal included gefilte fish, chicken soup and noodles, meat and side dishes such as sweet carrots (tzimmes), potatoes and noodle kugel. At the end of the meal we had compote for dessert. And as a final course we had tea with lemon accompanied by a cake, usually strudel. All this while we were singing songs of the Sabbath. Each one of us was given a chance to express himself in song, each child having his own favorite song. I always sung out of tune but my brother Aharon had an extraordinary voice. We would turn to him to ask, "Aharon, sing us a song," whereupon he would break into song and the whole family would join him. On the Sabbath day we again had a big meal which included chopped liver, calf's foot jelly and cholent. The cholent had been kept in the bakery from Friday and on the Sabbath day each family sent a member to bring their pot home.

According to one of the popular customs, Jewish boys who were conscripted to the Polish army would sneak into the bakery and gorge themselves on cholent from other people's pots as a gesture of protest.

At home we spoke mainly Yiddish and a little Hebrew. Hebrew we learned thanks to our reading the Holy Scriptures. We hardly spoke Polish, because of a decision by the Jews of the community to prevent the children from learning a foreign language and to insulate them as much as possible from the surrounding influence. The girls, on the other hand, knew Polish since they attended the regular public schools.

In our living room there was a big library case which held mainly religious books, the Babylonian Talmud, the Jerusalem Talmud, the Mishna, the writings of Rambam and various books written by rabbis of Hasidei Gur. Since my sisters borrowed books from friends, books by Shalom Aleichem, Y.L. Peretz, Shalom Asch and others began to appear in our house even though my parents clearly displayed their displeasure with these books. I very much enjoyed reading them, as well as the books on nature, geography and history that my brother Hershel brought home.

Journals in three languages also arrived at the house, including the Hebrew journal *HaHed* (The echo, a left-wing Israeli journal), which was sent occasionally by my brother Yosef from Hachshara.

In fact, as far back as I can remember my four older brothers, Yosef, Moshe, Hershel and Aharon, studied at yeshivas away from home. It was the custom then to send boys to yeshivas at the age of twelve or thirteen, close to bar mitzvah. My brothers were sent to the city where there were large Hasidic yeshivas. The Hasidic yeshivas employed newer educational methods and taught secular subjects in addition to the standard regular religious studies. The mobility between yeshivas was very great and often young boys went from yeshiva to yeshiva based on personal connections and differences in tuition and the level of the studies.

My oldest brother Yosef studied in a number of yeshivas when he was young, and then went for Hachshara training in the Poalei Agudat Yisrael near Vilna. There he began thinking about immigrating to Eretz Yisrael. My parents weren't happy about the idea and did not hide their objections. Their position reflected the position of the Hasidic rabbis, who thought that the attempt to immigrate to Eretz Yisrael was equivalent to trying to advance the coming of the Messiah and was therefore prohibited in principle. They were also afraid of the influence of the left-wing movements such as Poalei Zion Smol (the left-wing splinter group from Poalei Zion) or Hashomer Hatzair, which in their eyes stood for values that were foreign to Judaism.

Yosef did immigrate to Eretz Yisrael in 1935 despite the objections of my parents, and like many other pioneers worked for a period of time in building roads. In 1940 he married a young woman named Bracha and established a family. During most of the war years we managed to maintain contact with him through letters, and in the difficult days that came upon us we turned our eyes toward him and he shone like a lighthouse from the shores of the Promised Land.

Moshe, who was born after Yosef, joined the Hapoel Hamizrachi movement in Zeromin at the end of his studies at the yeshiva. In the framework of the movement, which believed in combining the Jewish religion with Zionism and socialism, he also planned to immigrate to Eretz Yisrael. But as fate would have it, he wasn't able to obtain a certificate to immigrate and since he had no choice he returned to Krasnosielc in 1939. Moshe lived with our parents, studied Torah at the *beit midrash* (house of study) and hoped to receive a certificate in a short time. In the summer of 1939, when the winds of war were already blowing in Europe, he became engaged to the daughter of a merchant but because of the historic events that overcame our area and all of Europe, he never married his betrothed.

Hershel studied at first in the Lodz Yeshiva and afterwards moved to another yeshiva in Warsaw, the capital, where he was exposed to the left-wing political influence that was common at the time. He stopped studying at the yeshiva and instead joined a socialist youth movement and began working at various jobs. My parents (especially my father) were not pleased with Hershel's life. The manner in which he chose his new life embarrassed them because it didn't fit in with Father's high status in the community. I didn't understand then what the commotion was about. In my eyes Hershel was a hero, and when he visited our home I enjoyed listening to his stories about what happened, about the movies he saw and the demonstrations he participated in. The socialist ideas that he talked about – the Friendship of Peoples, the World-Wide Solution – were pleasant to my ears even though I really didn't understand their meaning.

My brother Aharon also studied in a few yeshivas. In 1935 he went to my maternal grandfather's house in Serock and there began to study the trade of *shehitah*, but after six months he became sick with typhoid fever, which at the time was fatal. My father traveled to the Gerrer Rebbe to receive a blessing from him for Aharon – and surprisingly Aharon recovered almost immediately after receiving the blessing. But though he was considered less of a rebel than my older brothers, Aharon abandoned his studies as a *shohet* and returned home. Aharon was blessed with great intelligence, an unusual memory and a special sense of humor. Like my father, Aharon was among the Hasidim of the Gerrer Rebbe.

On holidays, my four older brothers would come for a visit. Our house filled with joy and chaos. From them we heard interesting stories of life in the yeshiva. And I, the younger boy, drank in their stories. I especially liked the stories of the visits to different houses each day within the framework of the tradition of *essen tag*. On these visits they got to know different customs and meet colorful types of people: prosperous businessmen alongside eccentrics and beggars. I became very emotional in anticipation of a visit from Hershel, who usually arrived for Passover. My curiosity was at a high pitch. I wanted to know all about his experiences: where he came from and where he was going. And I also wanted to understand the meaning of the storm that his visit raised in our home.

Because of my older brothers, I was exposed at home to the different political currents and the arguments they used. Already at the age of five I knew how to declaim, "Jabotinsky should be the minister of defense; Weizmann should be president." My earliest political memory was the hanging of Shlomo Bar Yosef, a Betar man who planned to carry out a terrorist attack on a bus in Rosh Pina. He was caught by the British and hanged in 1936. Hebrew and Yiddish newspapers covered the story. I read about the exchange of letters between him and his mother who lived in Lodz. In her letters she begged that he ask for a pardon but he stubbornly refused to do so. Despite my young age the events held me spellbound. For days my mind was consumed with admiration for Ben Yosef. In my mind I compared him to the heroic character of Bar Kochba whom I learned about in the heder. At this young age the seeds of the Zionist struggle for the rebirth of Jews in their own country were already planted in my mind. Little did I know then how significant a role this struggle would later take on in my own life.

In my childhood I stayed at home, mainly with my younger sister and brother. There were six of us still at home: Bronia, Leah, Yitshak, myself, Malka and Elimelech. My sisters never attended heder but sometimes a learned man would come to our house to teach them. At the age of six they began to attend a Polish public school. After six hours of school they then participated in auxiliary lessons in Judaism at Beit Yaakov. In their teens they also chose to learn a trade: Bronia learned sewing and Leah studied designing and sewing of women's lingerie.

Malka and Elimelech, my younger sister and brother, were very close to one another. I felt closest to my brother Yitshak who was only a little older then me. The ambivalent relations between us was evident from the mix of admiration and envy that we showed toward one another. We were very different from each other. Yitshak was practical and always stood up for himself while I was known as a compromiser, compliant and soft-hearted. He went around with his friends a lot, while I tried to be a good boy and obey my parent's wishes. He would sometimes dare to rebel against the iron religious discipline and was punished for it. I admired his courage but I also felt sorry that he was punished. In 1937 my brother Yitshak was sent to study in the yeshiva at Ostrolenka. I will never forget how he cried when the wagon came to take him to the yeshiva. But my parents didn't back down and were insistent that their children would be educated to independence. I was very worried about my own expected tranfer for studies at the yeshiva, while at the same time waiting impatiently for the occurrence.

Like all the sons in the family I began my official learning already at the age of three, when I started studying at the heder. Immediately after breakfast, which usually included a roll spread with butter, cheese and some pieces of herring for which I had a great fondness, we left for a long day of learning which ended at about 3:30 in the afternoon. Our group consisted of ten to fifteen pupils of about the same age. The discipline in the heder was quite strict: I still remember how one of the teachers used to beat us with a stick if we didn't learn our lessons or if we were late in returning from recess.

CHAPTER TWO

The War Begins

Suddenly on Friday, September 1, around three o'clock in the morning, the cannons thundered. The German Army crossed the border between Germany and Poland, at a distance of only about twenty-two miles from our town. Loud warnings came from the radio, which announced the beginning of the war and called citizens up for reserve duty. Many of the town's residents fled to towns and settlements that were at a distance from the border, hoping that the Polish army would halt the German forces before reaching them.

The Jews of the town were even more distressed, since they were forced to use the favors of the gentile coachmen. Rabbi Zilberberg fled with all his family to Makow Mazowiecki even before the Sabbath came in. His son-in-law, who had married his daughter not so long ago, was caught by the Germans and tied to galloping horses which tossed and shook him until he died.

That terrible Friday, fear and chaos descended upon our home. Six of my brothers and sisters were at my parents' home that day – my brother Moshe, who had completed his studies in the yeshiva and was waiting for his visa to immigrate to Palestine, Little Elimelech, my sisters Leah and Malka, Yitshak who came home from the yeshiva just two days ago and me.

The rest were absent – Yosef had left for Israel, Aharon was in his yeshiva, Hershel lived at that time in Warsaw and my sister Bronia was visiting my uncle Shalom, my mother's brother, in the town of Leczna.

Our heart urged us to flee somewhere safe, but no one knew where. Moreover, we were all convinced that we must flee from town as quickly as possible. My parents decided to pack some necessary personal belongings for the journey and leave other possessions hidden in the basement, especially items with sentimental value that we could not carry with us. There was a lot of commotion and tension was felt in the air. We hurried to complete all the chores before the Sabbath came in, as mother was not ready to give up the regular preparation of the Sabbath meal. We took our belongings to the basement, according to their order of importance – first all the books of the Babylonian Talmud, the Holy Scriptures and various books of Hasidism, then the new Singer sewing machine which was purchased for a lot of money about a month ago and was intended to be used by Bronia and Leah. We did not go to the synagogue, but mother insisted that we hold the Sabbath meal as usual.

The next morning, in spite of the sacredness of the Sabbath, my parents decided to send the little children Malka and Elimelech accompanied by Leah, our older sister, to our great grandfather's house in Serock. They also gave Leah the jewels and gifts purchased for Moshe's upcoming wedding. On Sabbath, at seven o'clock in the morning, the first bus left for Warsaw. Panic reigned among the residents of Krasnosielc as everyone tried to grab seats on the bus. After a lot of pushing the three succeeded to mount the bus.

In the afternoon my parents decided that there was no choice and the rest of the family members must also run away immediately. The destination was the town of Makow Mazowiecki which lay about fifteen miles away from us. It was a large town compared to our Krasnosielc, and therefore my father thought that it would be easier for us to hide there. My father, Moshe, Yitshak and myself started to walk, and in the evening we arrived at Makow and lodged in the rabbi's house.

In the meantime my mother, who was somewhat overweight and could not walk for long, had elected to remain behind. Shmuel Dovner, an acquaintance of my father's who knew Polish coach owners, agreed to make sure that she was driven to Makow Mazowiecki. The Sabbath was not over yet, but since the situation was life-threatening my mother agreed to leave on the Sabbath. But mid-journey the coachman suddenly stopped the carriage and announced that he was afraid to continue the ride, as many dangers lay in wait on the road. My mother was forced to dismount the carriage and pass the night in a close village. The next day she found her way back to Krasnosielc.

On Sunday, the Germans entered the town. The next day the butcher of Krasnosielc contacted my father and informed him that the Germans had asked the town's butchers to supply them with meat, but they refused to do so without the performance of the Jewish *shohet*. Therefore, the Germans ordered that the *shohet* be quickly brought back to town. My father immediately agreed to their request, mainly because he thought that my mother was waiting for us in town.

My brother Moshe was against returning back to our town. He was afraid of the dangers lying on the road. My father said, "You will not tell me what to do. I have known the Germans since the days of World War I. As long as there is turmoil on the roads, you can at least escape. Later, this will also be impossible."

So, father, Yitshak and I returned to Krasnosielc. Moshe and Aharon stayed in Makow, but a week later the Germans drove them away – they would never see my father again.

I will never forget the way back to Krasnosielc. We walked on the main road which led into town, while every now and then encountering German patrolmen who stopped us and asked for our documents. One time the soldiers searched our belongings and found a prayer shawl, phylacteries and a shofar. My father carried a shofar because of the approaching High Holidays Rosh Hashanah and Yom Kippur. The soldiers did not know, of course, what a shofar was and asked my father. He tried to explain to them in Yiddish and with broken German utterances, but one soldier suspected that the shofar was a signaling instrument, and that my father was in contact with members of the Polish military. He immediately ordered the three of us to stand by a tree, and two soldiers kneeled in front of us and prepared to shoot us. My father instructed us to recite the "Hear O Israel" before we died in sanctification of God's name. Our hearts were quivering with fear, but we followed his instructions. We murmured the prayer and waited for death. Like a miracle, a German officer appeared out of nowhere riding a motorcycle. He asked the soldiers what was going on and they reported. After a few minutes the officer yelled toward us, "*Heraus, heraus* (Move on, move on)" and with his hand ordered us to leave the place. One moment we were standing against inevitable death and the next we continued walking. The memory of this incident will stay with me forever.

We continued walking, overwhelmed with fear. German military forces were continually passing us on their way into the center of Poland.

We arrived home on Tuesday evening, where Mother was impatiently waiting for us. The atmosphere was dreary and heavy. German soldiers were all over town, and curfew was declared. The Jewish people were prohibited to leave their homes during the evening hours. Rumors were whispered in our ears, to our utmost terror, that the Germans had murdered the other *shohet* in town because they had found a *shehitah* knife among his possessions. When the Jewish townsmen were informed of my father's return, many people gathered in our home, trying to inculcate confidence in each other. Some people, the Hasidim of the Gerrer Rebbe, tried to cheer each other up with the Rebbe's words. "This is the year 5700 [in Hebrew this spells the verb 'exhaust']," they said, clinging to their faith. "Therefore Satan's power will be exhausted and the Germans will suffer military defeat."

The next morning, Wednesday, September 5, 1939 (22 Elul, 5700), German soldiers went through town and recruited all men, both Jewish and Polish. The Germans announced that they needed men for the reconstruction of the town's bridge. The Polish military bombed the bridge while trying to delay the advancement of the Germans. My father and his friends went up to hide in our attic. Shortly later, a few soldiers entered our home. Some started to search for money, valuables or any evidence of so-called hostile Jewish intentions toward Germans. We could see the burning hate in their eyes. I believe that the men's sidelocks and beards inflamed their hate even more. One soldier took a citron box out of the wardrobe. Together with his friends, as if amused by a children's game, he threw the box toward us. The box hit my jaw and broke my front teeth. My mother immediately ordered me to stop crying, so that the soldiers' attention would not be drawn to me. A few soldiers went up to the attic, where they found my father and his friends covered with prayer shawls and phylacteries. Shouting and cursing, the soldiers dragged them out and took them away with them.

Around two o'clock in the afternoon, my father came suddenly back and told us that the Germans sent him and other Jewish people to bring food for their friends. My mother begged him to find a place to hide and not to go back to the Germans. My father refused. He explained that the Germans had threatened them that if they did not return they would shoot ten or twelve other Jewish people instead. His conscience did not let him run away, but he tried to calm my mother down, saying that the Germans had promised him and his friends that they would be back home before curfew began. Prior to leaving home, he looked for a prayer book in order to recite the confession. Who knows, maybe in the depth of his heart he knew that he would never return.

Approximately an hour and a half later, my father left home equipped with pots filled with food prepared by my mother. I accompanied him. We walked together, stopping just one street before the bridge. Before leaving, my father bent toward me, kissed me on my cheek and said, "Take care of Mother. I do not know what will happen. They abuse us. They spit on us."

I did not understand why he made me responsible to take care of my mother and why she should need my protection. What could I do? I was only a nine-and-a-half-year-old child. I returned home with a heart full of questions and concerns. Due to my young age and my extreme innocence I could not have even imagined that I would never see him again.

After the curfew started, the evening hours passed by one after the other, and the men never came home. Night fell. Fear crept into the hearts of the women, and some of them even dared to risk the curfew and leave their homes to find out where their husbands were. Residents living by the synagogue told them that they heard the sound of shootings coming from the synagogue during the night.

The next morning my mother and a few other women ran to the synagogue to find out what had happened, but guards of German soldiers who were placed there did not let them in. They went to the German town major and asked about the fate of their husbands. The officer answered that the German military recruited them to do additional repair jobs in other places.

Two days later, the guard left the synagogue and the terrified women broke in and found that their worst fears had materialized. The furniture and the benches were knocked onto the floor. The walls had bullet holes in them and blood stains were seen all over the place, although it seemed that someone had tried hard to cover them up. Nevertheless, at this early point of the war no one even conceived of the possibility of a mass murder.

In the meantime, my brothers Moshe, Aharon and Elimelech and my sisters Malka and Leah came back to town. Soon the High Holidays were upon us. We hardly left the house, and we even avoided attending the synagogue. People who came to our home to recite the *Slihot* prayers (confessional prayers recited in the weeks preceding Yom Kippur, the Day of Atonement) conversed with each other quietly and with heavy hearts, fearing the unknown. Indeed, the harassments stopped, but the atmosphere was bleak. In retrospect, it became clear that after the synagogue incident the commander of the local German force had gathered his troops and ordered them to restrain themselves.

On the eve of Sukkot, October 1939, our neighbor Kozica came to our house early in the morning. Kozica sold bread to the Germans and therefore found out ahead of everyone else what the Germans were plotting. She told us that the Germans were about to deport us from the town. And indeed, a few hours later the German soldiers went from house to house and ordered all the Jewish residents to gather a few clothes and other necessary items and to assemble in the town square at eight o'clock in the morning. My mother took over. We started to pack various belongings in sheets and tied their ends. We gathered clothes, utensils and food, two slaughtered geese and a little flour. In addition, we took pillows and warm blankets with us to protect ourselves from the expected cold. I remember the scene very well – there was noise and tumult everywhere and our two-year-old Elimelech who had just started to speak ran all over the place and announced with his soft voice: "I already have my pillow. We can leave."

My mother, who did not forsake her faith then or during the hard days that would follow, took our Bible with her.

When we arrived at the square, we saw many carriages with horses around it and gentile coachmen recruited by the Germans. On the stage sat a German officer and a man called Gotfried Richter, a town resident of German origin, a *Volks Deutsche*, who had been appointed by the

Germans to be the town's mayor. They made speeches in which we were ordered to choose one of the following possibilities: "As hard times befell you and no one knows what is in store for you, and as the military and the municipality will not be able to protect you," they said, "you now have two possibilities. Whoever wants to stay in town can do that, but it will be his sole responsibility, as later it will be impossible to leave. On the other hand, whoever wishes to leave town will sign that he does so of his own free will. He can have a horse and a carriage and will be permitted to travel toward the Russian forces."

In retrospect we understood the choice the Germans offered us. In August 1939, Nazi Germany and the USSR signed the Molotov-Ribbentrop Pact, which ensured that they would not attack each other. Ironically, the pact paved the way for the beginning of World War II. The pact had confidential appendices, one of which contained an agreement to divide Poland between Germany and Russia. The Germans and the Russians activated the treaty and Poland was divided. The Bug, one of Poland's largest rivers, was designated as the border limit between the two countries.

Behind this fabricated "humane gesture" of the Germans lay their wish to get rid of Jewish people from our town and throughout Poland. In October 1939, during the first days of the war, the Germans had not yet activated their plot of the mass destruction of the European Jewish people, and apart from occasional murders, such as the one which had taken place in the town's synagogue, they tried to "cleanse" the area by deporting Jewish people to Soviet-ruled areas.

All the Jews in town "chose" to leave, our family included. Later it became clear that fate had smiled on us, because the people who were not deported were transferred to ghettos and later sent to concentration camps to be murdered.

At the end of the town-square speech, all the Jews left the place in dozens of carriages. During the departure, the Germans made the adults sign forms, according to which they were leaving town of their own free will. For one reason or other it was still important for the Germans to make a good impression. At the same time they ordered the deportees to leave behind all their gold and silver coins as well as their foreign currency.

We all left, my mother and her seven children in one carriage, heading east. On the way, the Polish coachmen threatened us that if we did not give them money or gold jewelry, they would leave us behind. We did not have money, neither did we have jewelry; therefore my mother was forced to give them some of our pillows and blankets. The coachmen did not have any problem taking the pillows and blankets from us, although they knew that we were headed for a long journey and would be susceptible to the cold of the approaching winter. My mother, with her gift of resourcefulness, convinced them to leave some of the pillows and blankets with us, which in the long run turned out to be lifesavers.

During the ride I suffered from very bad indigestion, probably because of the stress. I did not want to bother my family members and I did not tell any of them about it. I tried to overcome the problem by myself, but it caused me a lot of discomfort and suffering. At night, we arrived at the town Rozan, and we spent the night on the floor of an abandoned Polish military camp. At dawn, we saw that there were fresh heaps of soil around us with wooden crosses on them. A helmet punctured with holes was placed on each cross. It did not take us long to understand that it was the graveyard of many Polish soldiers killed there just a few days before. The sense of being surrounded by death intensified and became stronger minute by minute.

That day we started a bonfire and roasted our geese. We packed the leftovers and took them with us. The coachmen who led us from Krasnosielc had already returned home, so we hired other coachmen to lead us to Ostrow Mazowiecki. When we arrived there, we understood that the Germans had preceded us. We stayed there a few days, and during the nights we found shacks, where we stretched out on the floor our warm blankets and pillows and lay down to sleep. Though only October, the nights were already very cold.

German soldiers dressed up in fine clothes occasionally passed us. They wore scarves on their necks and their hands were covered with white gloves. They wore elegant hats with drawings of human skulls. They walked peacefully and pleasantly and their hands were crossed behind their backs. It was the first time in my life that I beheld SS officers. Their piercing, hate-filled looks made a deep and lasting impression on me. Fear overwhelmed me, and each time I was absolutely sure that they were about to seal our fate. A few minutes later they would leave the place, and I would breathe a deep sigh of relief.

After a few days' stay in Ostrow, the Germans announced that all the refugees had to leave town immediately. The townsmen worried about crowdedness and about diseases brought upon them by refugees, and they determined to deport us. We decided to try and advance toward the area ruled by the Russians. Moshe, the oldest, went outside the town's borders and found a carriage. We all mounted the carriage and loaded the few belongings we had. Exhausted and dispirited we went on our way again. This time we headed toward Zambrow, a town just inside the Russian border. Later, it became clear that fortune was smiling on us again. Eyewitnesses told us that a few days after we had left Ostrow, the Germans summoned the remaining Jews to the town square and shot them indiscriminately. About five hundred Jews were murdered that day. The Germans hurried to bury them in a mass grave while some were still breathing. According to later testimonies, the earth kept moving for a long time after. I suffered from terrible nightmares for days after.

In the meantime, we went on with our journey. I again suffered from bad indigestion. The border line that separated the area ruled by the Germans from that ruled by the Russians crossed about two miles from Zambrow. When we arrived at the Russian area we met Soviet soldiers for the first time. I remember that I was very impressed by their uniforms. The officers wore flat hats and boots, and the soldiers wore navy hats and leggings. Red stars, the symbols of the Communist country, ornamented all the hats. For some reason, I remember a strong scent of a mixture of cabbage and diesel fuel coming from the military kitchens. The Soviet soldiers welcomed us in a friendly way and even served us soup. They even had a few soldiers of Jewish origin, and we were happy to speak Yiddish with them. For a moment it seemed that we had finally left the valley of death and from now on everything would be fine. Yet my mother, who had heard many stories of rape, ransacking and pogroms performed by the Russians during World War I, repeatedly warned us. She called the Russians *borwese*, which means "bare-footed" in Yiddish, because during the revolution they walked with bare feet and she unequivocally claimed that they were even worse than the Germans.

Like us, many other Jewish refugees arrived in Zambrow, Slonim, Stolin and other towns. Upon arrival they looked for relatives and acquaintances who might accommodate them. As a family blessed with children we were given an apartment of our own in Zambrow. We lived there for only a few days until the end of October 1939, when we were deported in disgrace. We later found out that most of the townsmen of Krasnosielc arrived in Slonim – only to be cold-bloodedly murdered by the Germans following the town's invasion.

As the residents of Zambrow started to fear the crowdedness and diseases which could be caused by the arrival of the refugees, we were ordered to leave town. We decided to continue to Bialystok. It was a larger city and had a committee that took care of Jewish affairs. The Jewish community in Zambrow borrowed trucks from the Russian military, in which they transported the women and children to Bialystok. The trucks were overcrowded and, with great sorrow, my mother had to leave behind the Bible she had carried with her from Krasnosielc. Due to lack of space, the men could not mount the trucks and they had to make their own way to Bialystok. They walked to the town Czyzow, where they mounted the train to Bialystok.

We arrived at Bialystok in October 1939. The Jewish committee temporarily housed the large number of refugees in different buildings in town. We were sent to the main synagogue, one of the two synagogues in town. Women, men and children crowded together. We stayed in the synagogue approximately two weeks in crowded conditions, noise and tumult. Due to the holy atmosphere of the place, we went out to the yard to cook on Primus stoves.

About two weeks after we arrived at Bialystok, my brother Hershel suddenly showed up. He had come all the way from Warsaw on his own after he had participated in the city's defense. Hershel told us that after two weeks of long resistance and the death of many people, Poland's capital had been conquered by the Germans. Hershel took upon himself to take care for the family. He found a room for us in Botonicna Street, not far from the railway station. It was a little room in an old shack which was subdivided into a number of rooms and furnished with a few pieces of furniture collected from the street. We were ten people crowded into this shack, suffering from terrible winter cold and strong summer heat. Nevertheless, we blessed our good fortune and the fact that we had a place to live. Our rent was relatively low, and we lived in the shack for more than six months, during the entire period of our stay in Bialystok.

Approximately one month after arriving to Bialystok, my sister Bronia also joined us. She came to us on her own dressed up like a Polish country girl. She told us that on the way she had met someone from Krasnosielc and when she had asked him how we were, he had turned his back on her and had not responded. She had become afraid that something horrible had happened to us, but when she found out that we had fled eastward she made her way to Bialystok, where all of us were more than happy to reunite. Now we were almost all together. We missed only Yosef, who had left to Palestine, and father, whose fate we did not know.

We started to feel at home in Bialystok – mainly because of my brother Hershel, who was a very practical person and took things into his own hands. The other brothers were yeshiva students and did not know how to cope with stressful situations as well as he did. Hershel took Aharon and together they started to trade in various products. Every day they went out to the market to sell saccharin cubes which were used as sugar substitutes. After a while, Hershel decided that Yitshak and I had to carry the burden of support as well and that we had to join them and work, too. For me it was a significant change, because as a religious child I had never imagined that I would have to go out there and work at such a young age. Hershel promised that when times changed and things were as before, we would be able to return to our former way of life, to religion and to studying, but at that time we did not have any choice but to work and earn our bread. I accepted his words without dispute. In addition, he suggested that in order not to draw unnecessary attention from the government, it would be better if we cut our sidelocks and changed our traditional clothes to more modern clothes. He took us to the barber, who cut our sidelocks, and he bought us peak caps, which made our appearance look as authentic Gentile boys. Although I did not totally understand the significance of his actions and their motives, I trusted him with all my heart, and regarded him as a wise and practical adult. I was very thankful that he took upon himself the burden of responsibility for our safety and well-being.

Hershel introduced me to a Jew, who put in my hands a few bags with saccharin cubes every morning, when I went out to the large and roofed market in Bialystok. I ran among the people passing by and cried out "saccharin, saccharin." Every now and then people talked to me in Russian, Polish or Yiddish and asked to buy some saccharin. Government and medical control was imposed on saccharin in those days and its sale was prohibited. Therefore Hershel trained me that if I saw an inspector or a policeman I would have to run very fast, and indeed, every time I encountered policemen and inspectors I ran away from them as fast as I could. I was fortunate enough never to be caught. Apart from saccharin I also sold Damska cigarettes, which were long and elegant cigarettes for women. Thus I ran around many hours every day, from dawn to dusk. Often I went out to the market when the weather was bad. Then it was very cold and the snow piled up on my shoulders. In the evening I returned home exhausted and went straight to bed. I gave my mother the money I earned and once in a while I bought different products in the market, according to her request. It amazed us how my mother ran the household in the small shack we lived in, and up to this day I do not understand how she cooked meals for all of us – ten people – on that little Primus stove. During the whole period of our stay in Bialystok, we made sure, mostly because of my mother, to follow the traditional laws of Judaism, especially the rules of keeping kosher and the sanctity of the Sabbath.

I worked very hard, but I was pleased that I met all the challenges I took upon myself and I was proud of my contribution to the family's support. The stress that accompanied me every day only encouraged me to continue, as did Hershel's socialist speeches, delivered to me and my brothers, about the importance of every man working in order to support himself. For me it was a sharp and dramatic change in my way of thinking. In contrast to the passivity promoted in my childhood, Hershel taught us to take responsibility over our fate. I was very proud that I, too, who was not yet ten years old, could be useful to myself and to others. To this day I am thankful to my brother Hershel who gave me a practical perspective at such a young age and inspired me with self-respect.

The other brothers also worked to support the family. My sister Leah worked in a chocolate factory and brought home candies as well as money. My brother Yitshak sold clothes and the others helped every now and then, especially with cutting the saccharin cubes to small crystals. Bronia, our oldest sister, stayed at home and helped mother. We worked hard and all of us chipped in to ease the burden, but like in every family, we, too, had our arguments.

Our living conditions were harsh and, like other refugees, we became ill with various diseases. Malka suffered from pneumonia, my mother had a certain disease in her digestive system, and my brother Moshe became infected with typhoid and was admitted to the hospital for a long time. He recovered, but could not recuperate from the weakness he felt.

During that time we did not know what had become of our father. In our hearts we continued to hope that the rumors about the murder in the synagogue were baseless and that Father was alive, and one day he would join us as Hershel and Bronia had done. In November 1939 Hershel met a Jew called Moshe Albrish who had also been summoned to repair the bridge; Moshe told Hershel how our father had been murdered. He told Hershel how the Germans had ordered the Jewish and Polish men to carry heavy logs of wood in the turbulent waters of the river. Two or three older men who could not withstand the hard work were immediately shot and their bodies were thrown into the river. Others were beaten and cursed throughout the work. When the job was over, the Germans ordered the workers to stand in two separate groups, Jewish and Polish. Some of the Jews who looked more modern managed to infiltrate the Polish group and thus saved themselves from the fate that befell their friends. The rest, who looked typically Jewish, were brought to the synagogue in town. The soldiers ordered them to sit on the benches close to the eastern wall and started to mock them: "If your God is omnipotent, pray to Him and let us see if He will save you." Some soldiers pulled the beards of the Jews till their chins bled. The abuse took a while until some soldiers suddenly aimed flashlights toward the helpless men. They placed machine guns in front of them and started to shoot at them indiscriminately and mercilessly. The victims started to cry out, "Hear O Israel" until their voices were no more. The Germans stopped, checked how many had been killed and immediately started to shoot again.

They stopped shooting when another German military unit burst into the place, headed by an officer who was a doctor, dressed in white. He ordered the soldiers to stop, approached the Jews and checked who was alive. Seven men, who had been shielded by the bodies of their friends, were injured and were pulled out of the heap. The German officer ordered to give them first aid and transfer them in an ambulance to the military hospital in Olstyn, Germany. The injured men received medical care in the hospital, but two of them died a few hours later. The remaining five were treated and released from the hospital. We understood from Moshe Albrish that our father had died immediately.

Although listening to the story with great sorrow, some of the facts still seemed to us clearly improbable. Why did the Germans decide to murder the Jews who were innocent of any crime? Why was the shooting suddenly stopped? Why were the injured men brought to a German hospital, of all places, for treatment? We found it hard to believe. Later on, when I thoroughly research the incident, the conclusions showed absurd circumstances and the bitter scorn of fate. But at the time we clung to these doubts in the hope that the story was basically unfounded. However, the pain of loss started to creep into our hearts.

During that period we renewed our contacts with my brother Yosef in Palestine. He used to send us food packages through the American Jewish Joint Distribution Committee, which helped us greatly. In one of her letters to Yosef, mother described the story of Moshe Albrish. Yosef, who was of course shocked by the story, sent the letter to the newspaper (I do not remember whether it was *Hatzofeh* or *Hamodia*) and it was published in Hebrew. Dozens of years later, I accidentally found the letter, translated into Hebrew, in a book published by Shlomo Carmeli, a Jew from Krasnosielc who immigrated to Palestine in the twenties.

On Passover Eve, at the end of the prayer in the synagogue, the rabbi asked the residents of Bialystok to invite refugees to their homes for the Seder. One of the townsmen approached me and invited me to his home, which I gladly accepted. I will never forget that Seder. All the family members sat around a clean and festively organized table. A white tablecloth was spread over it and delicious holiday dishes were served in shining utensils. Six months had passed since all our family members had sat for a festive meal, and the memory seemed to belong to another world and another life. I thanked God for letting me taste again of the beautiful things in life, but my thoughts wandered to the Seder table in my parents' home. I wondered if all of us would ever sit again around one table.

In spite of the hospitality that night, most of the members of the Bialystok Jewish community, a large and organized community, did not like the fact that Jewish refugees had "invaded" their city. They claimed that the refugees were a burden on the community. They took over their institutions and brought in diseases such as typhoid and lice. Some God-fearing Jewish people claimed that such a fate had befallen us because we had sinned more than they had. Later it became clear that their destiny, like the destiny of most of the Jewish people in Bialystok, was even worse than ours.

We, the refugees, used to reach out to each other and divide among ourselves the little that we had. We met with each other frequently, helped each other and gave advice to each other. It seemed that the uncertainty of the future, the poverty and the harsh conditions – they were the causes of our unity.

In the meantime, the Soviet government also started to take steps to get rid of the refugees. They confiscated property and whoever was marked as a threat was exiled to Siberia. The capital owners were exiled first, followed by the members of the Bund and finally the religious people. In July 1940, every family was asked to declare what it intended to do at the end of the war. Does it intend to return to Fascist Poland, to immigrate to Palestine or the United States, or perhaps stay in the USSR and take a part in building the homeland? Those who chose the last possibility were considered as the ones with the "right" decisions and were sent to big cities such as Kiev, Dniepropetrowsk or Smolensk to participate in developing the Russian industry. Others who chose to immigrate to Palestine or the United States were considered as having Fascist views and were exiled to Siberia, where they were sentenced to hard physical labor under conditions of cold and hunger; many of them would never return. On the other hand, people who chose to stay in Poland were considered as having harmless yearnings for their homeland. They were sent to European Siberia, which was considered "softer." Most refugees, including my family, chose that possibility. Hershel, who had the right certificates, was allowed to continue and engage in trade, and therefore we all believed that his fate would be better than ours. Two days before we were expelled, Hershel went out as usual to trade in Slonim. He stood next to the truck and waved us goodbye. We could not imagine that we would never see him again.

On Saturday morning, about nine months after arriving to Bialystok, the NKVD showed up and forced us to mount the trucks. We traveled to the town's railway station to start our journey to Siberia – packing again, moving on again. We took with us the little that we had for the way, but we were forced to give up even that when we arrived at the railway station.

Because of rumors that the Soviet government intended to hunt down men who did not have passports, Aharon and Moshe found a hiding place in the attic of an acquaintance's house, but the members of the NKVD found them. Aharon showed them his passport, but the officer ordered both to join us in the railway station: "You do not need a passport in the place you are going to. You will find a job there even without a passport." His words were only too true.

CHAPTER THREE

Survival in Siberia

Thousands of refugees, both Jews and Gentiles, were forced into the Bialystok railway station that Sabbath morning of July 1940. The NKVD policemen shouted at us to board the train cars. They pushed the refugees toward the benches without listening to what they had to say. People were desperately searching for each other and loud cries echoed through the railway station.

Mother, Bronia, Leah and Malka, Moshe, Aharon, Yitshak, Elimelech and I boarded the train. It was designed to transport cargo, with long benches installed inside each car. The train was so crowded that we could hardly move. All passengers looked up at the tiny hatches that let some air into the compartment.

When morning came we saw that we had arrived in White Russia. The train continued until it stopped in Minsk. We had made the long journey without bathroom facilities, and when the train stopped people hurried off the train and relieved themselves in front of each other in spite of themselves. A Russian soldier who was watching the embarrassing scene entered the train and dug a large hole in its floor with an axe. We hung a blanket around the open hole to protect the privacy of the passengers as much as possible. This was a true relief, as the journey took about a month to complete.

The train continued on its way north. Every now and then it stopped for short breaks, during which we got off the train and stretched our legs. We could not walk much, as it was terribly cold and we preferred to hide under our warm blankets. At each stop, the NKVD representative gave us boiling water (*kipyatok*, in Russian) and tiny portions of bread, potatoes and rice, which was really not enough to diminish our hunger. There were no cooking facilities on the train for the whole journey. The crowded and harsh conditions during the trip caused the spread of diseases among the passengers.

A month later we arrived in the town of Kotlas where the railroad track came to an end. When we stepped off the train we were given a fish soup called *treska*, which smelled bad because it was cooked from rotten fish. Due to the circumstances we could not allow ourselves to be choosy and we ate the soup with great appetite. When we finished, we boarded a *barka*, which was a large, square barge pulled by a steamship, and we started to go northward along the Vichegda River (near the Pieczora River). Hundreds of people were crowded in the *barka* under harsh conditions, but fortunately, in contrast to the train, here we could enjoy the water and the restrooms.

The *barka* brought us to Ostwim, which lay in the northern region of Komi. In the past, this area had been populated by Eskimos from the Komi tribe, and upon our arrival it was still possible to meet some of the descendants of the Komi tribe who looked like Mongolians. The rest of the residents in the region were Russians and Ukrainians who came there after being deported following the revolution during the years 1919–1921 and during the period of agricultural collectivization in the thirties. These were citizens who were considered by the government as counter-revolutionaries. Among them were religious people, members of the bourgeois and farmers. Here the government had erected Gulags – large labor camps whose purpose was to reeducate prisoners accused of political or civil crimes. We, on the other hand, were considered "harmless" refugees and were to be sent to residential villages rather than to hard labor camps. As it soon became clear, the life in these villages was not at all easy.

On Friday we boarded trucks and continued our journey. Even then Mother did not give up lighting candles on Friday. While traveling, Aharon prepared a "paper cigarette" which she lit for a few seconds, and thus she could keep the tradition.

A few hours later we arrived at the very isolated village of Kiltowo. The railroad tracks did not reach the village, vehicles only occasionally came there and it took a lot of effort to travel to neighboring settlements. A river which was used by the locals for transportation of wooden logs ran close to Kiltowo. In the summer they transported the logs in boats and in the winter the logs were carried on vehicles which traveled on the frozen river, which had a layer of ice three feet thick. Almost all the residents of the area worked in preparing wooden logs for shipment and transport over the rivers toward the Baltic Sea.

In the village the dozens of Jewish families who arrived with us from Poland and Lithuania were given wooden residential homes. The locals welcomed us kindly and showed us how to insulate our houses from the cold with a certain weed which grew in the region. They gave us additional advice on how to protect our lives under the harsh weather conditions. The house had wooden benches used for sleeping. On these benches we placed mattresses made of the weed and covered ourselves with our warm blankets. We used the *pieczka*, the brick wood stove, for both cooking and heating. A soft light came from the electrical bulbs installed in the room. We took showers at the public bath house in the village.

A day or two after we arrived in Kiltowo, Krawcejew, the NKVD officer who was in charge of the village, gathered us together. Everyone nicknamed him *Zombal* ("The Tooth Owner," in Russian) because of his protruding front teeth.

"Comrades, as the palm of my hand will never grow hair, you will never see Poland again," said the officer from the goodness of his heart. "Your mission is to survive here, and it depends only on you. We do not care whether you survive or not. Our country is large and we have enough refugees." Later on, Zombal sent the men and women to work and the children to school.

Apart from a few skilled people, such as carpenters, tailors, shoemakers and hatters who remained working in the village, most men were assigned to work in the woods. The assignments were diverse – tree felling, cutting thin branches, hauling trees to the river and chopping them for heating or steam production. Most women were engaged in less-strenuous jobs such as cleaning the areas where the trees were cut down and burning small branches. The workers were divided into "brigades," each of which was headed by a "brigadier." The men got up early and had to work as many hours as necessary to complete the work quota. The quantity of food they received depended on their output. Most Jewish people were not used to hard physical labor and it was very difficult for them to hold on.

Aharon and Moshe were also sent to work in the woods. Every morning they were given a saw, a shovel and an axe and then they went into the woods to cut down trees. After the tree clearing they had to cut the branches, split the trunk into a number of pieces and pull the tree to the river bank on sleds. Bronia was at first also assigned to work in the woods, but a short time later she was sent to the same kind of work in a different forest. My sister Leah was assigned to Zombal's office.

Yitshak, Malka, Elimelech and I were too young to work. Elimelech, the youngest, was sent to a kindergarten and we, to school. We studied literature, mathematics, history, Marxism, geography, nature and the Russian language and we had gymnastics every day. At first I could not understand a word of Russian, but it did not take me too long to learn to speak the language. I adapted to the studying environment very quickly and became one of the best students in class. My grades were excellent and my teachers were continuously complimenting me. I was also appreciated by my friends who were always asking questions and copying my homework.

The children of the NKVD officers had better conditions than we, the refugee children. They were given large warm scarves and wore pretty hats and white boots. Unlike us, they always had very large sandwiches, occasionally with pieces of meat. Although they evoked my jealousy, their presence inspired me with hope. I was happy to know that there were better lives than mine, and hoped that maybe one day I would also be lucky enough to live that kind of life.

During our entire stay in Kiltowo we suffered from a constant food shortage. Although we were given basic food products, such as flour, some margarine and foul-tasting bread, the size of the portion depended on the effort we put into the work we were assigned to. The people who worked hard were given larger portions than sick people and children. We had not tasted meat, fruit, butter, salt or sugar for a long time. During our first days in Kiltowo we enjoyed the saccharine we brought with us from Bialystok, and we could even support ourselves a little from selling it, but those days quickly ended. A short time after our arrival we planted potatoes in the garden of our house, as it was one of the few vegetables that could grow in such a harsh climate. We gathered them at the end of summer so that the first frost would not damage them and in the winter we kept them in cloth-covered bags and boxes to prevent them from freezing. My mother tried all the time to get some more food for us, and often prepared things out of almost nothing. For example, we bought sardines from local fishermen from which she prepared gefilte fish. She made latkes out of the potatoes we grew. In the autumn we picked mushrooms after we learned how to distinguish between eatable and poisonous ones. In the spring we picked berries. To overcome the shortage in vitamins we used to eat various herbs. In the autumn we picked nettle after we found out that it was rich in vitamins. My mother boiled it a few times in order to get rid of the bitter taste. We drank the water soaked with vitamins and from the nettle itself my mother prepared "delicacies."

In Elimelech's kindergarten the children were given a certain quantity of sugar, and the kindergarten teacher said that if they spilled a little sugar, they were not allowed to pick it up from the table by themselves. Three-year-old Elimelech discovered a smart trick. He wet a glass and placed it on the dispersed sugar. Later, when no one was watching, he used to lick the bottom of the glass with the sugar grains sticking to it and became the happiest child.

One day, when I went out to the woods to gather berries and mushrooms, I lost my way. I was frightened and started to cry and yell for help in Yiddish and Russian. I yelled "help!" over and over again, but with no use. I felt completely helpless, but in spite of the weakness overcoming me, I did not let go of the berry bucket. The silence in the woods made the sounds of the different animals – birds, squirrels and hares – much louder. I could hear the howling of jackals and wolves and in my imagination I saw predators waiting for me at every corner. I wandered around the woods for about two to three hours, all the while crying for help. Suddenly I saw in front of me a man with a thick beard and a shotgun in his hand. I was terrified. I thought that he was going to shoot me but he calmed me down, patted my head and invited me to his nearby shack. It turned out that the man was a Provoslavic priest who had been exiled to Siberia by the government. He lived alone in the woods, worked as a forester and earned his living as a hunter. When we arrived at the shack I saw animal skins and horns hanging on the walls and a huge library with books on religion. The forester gave me hot fish soup and bread, and when he heard that I was a Jewish boy from Poland, he said: "You Jews are a smart people. You introduced us to the Bible and to other major doctrines, and we appreciate you very much for that, but at the same time, you also made some mistakes. You introduced Jesus to the world, and as a result a lot of blood was shed – Jewish, Provoslavic,

Lutheran and Catholic. Later on you introduced us to Marx and many died because of him. I also suffered because of him. I will give you a very important piece of advice, and if you ever make it out of here alive please pass it on to influential Jewish people in the world. First test your ideas in a country established by you for the Jewish people and then disseminate it to the rest of the world. Do not hurry to sell us ideas and let us shed our blood for an additional thousands of years, because that will make us hate you." When he ended his speech, the forester escorted me back to Kiltowo and we separated. I thanked him from the bottom of my heart for his help.

The spirit of the forester's speech penetrated deep into my heart, although I did not completely understand it. Later on, I counted it as my first Zionist experience.

As long as the weather was relatively comfortable, our main concern was to satiate our hunger. Yet when the cold set in our thoughts focused on warming our bodies and our homes. The winter was terrible in these regions. Heavy snow was already falling in September and reached a height of six feet. The temperatures went quickly down to forty degrees below zero. We tried to wear as many layers of clothing as possible and on top of these we wore a kind of cotton coat with more layers made from a plant used for insulation. We covered our ears with cotton hats. We were mostly worried about our feet. To warm those up we squeezed newspapers and socks into our felt shoes.

We made sure to rub our body parts in the snow in order to accelerate the blood flow and prevent freezing. We learned that under no circumstances should one sit outside without moving, as one could freeze to death through such behavior. When blood flow is slowed, the body's warning systems signaling danger are damaged and a feeling of comfort sets in, accompanied by pleasant hallucinations. Sometimes we were tempted to surrender to that "sweet death." It happened to me, too, but I was lucky because someone saw my condition and saved my life.

In the winter the sun set around three o'clock in the afternoon and rose only many hours later, but we went to sleep early in the afternoon in any case as sleep was the most effective cure for hunger. In the summer, on the other hand, the sun set around nine o'clock in the evening and at two o'clock in the morning it rose again. But in the summer we were struck by another problem: mosquitoes. We suffered from them terribly throughout the summer.

Because of the harsh conditions there were many diseases in that region. I first became ill with tetanus, which can do serious damage to the nervous system, and later suffered for a whole year from night blindness, caused by the lack of vitamins. My teeth started to wobble around, and I found it difficult to chew bread because my gums were weakening. At night I could not see anything except weak light spots which were cast by the lamp. The fact that I could not do my homework during the night hours bothered me a lot, as I had to complete them during the few hours of light. My mother who took care of me during my illness went to seek the advice of the village paramedic, who told her to make me drink castor oil or cod-liver oil, but she either did not believe in the effectiveness of these oils or just could not get ahold of them.

One day a man with torn and patched clothes knocked on our shack door. My mother asked him who he was and he answered, "I ran away from solitary confinement and I am looking for a place to spend the night." My mother knew that hiding such a man could cause us to be severely punished. She hesitated. Suddenly the man noticed that I used the wall for support while walking around the room. He turned to my mother and said: "If you let me sleep here under the bed, I will cure your child." The man told her that he had a small bottle of cod-liver oil in case he would be struck with night blindness, since this was the tested medicine for that illness. He promised my mother that if I drank a few tablespoons of the oil during the night, I would be able to see again the next day. My mother agreed and he gave me the drops of oil to swallow. In the morning I excitedly announced, "Mama, I can see!" But the man had disappeared at sunrise and mother decisively ruled: "There is no doubt that Elijah the Prophet visited us."

As the communist philosophy opposed religion, both Jewish people and Christians were prohibited to maintain a religious lifestyle. Nevertheless, most Jews continued to pray and practice their religion secretly. We arrived in Kiltowo shortly before the High Holidays, and Moshe and Aharon wished to be released from work in order to commemorate them, especially Yom Kippur. Aharon approached Dr. Spielman, a doctor who had traveled with us in the train and was appointed the village's local doctor. He authorized Aharon's release from working on Rosh Hashanah and Moshe's release from working on Rosh Hashanah and Yom Kippur. When my mother later became sick because of the cold and hunger, Dr. Spielman also helped her.

He ordered to have her admitted to the local hospital, thereby saving her life.

On Yom Kippur a Jew named Levinson was in charge of the prayer. During his sermon he encouraged people by claiming: "As the Jewish people withstood Pharaoh, Nebuhadnezzar and the Inquisition, so shall we withstand the Russians, as the Lord is with us." The Russians, who were informed about his sermon, accused Levinson of preaching against the Communist regime. He was given a trial and received a three-year sentence. Other Jewish people, who participated in the prayer, too, were punished and sent to prison, and the rest were reprimanded and warned not to participate in such a prayer again.

In spite of the prohibition and the danger it entailed, my mother continued to light candles every Friday night. As wax candles were not available, she used to light oil candles. She had never given up on reading *Tzena Ur'ena* ("Go Forth And Behold," a book written in Yiddish for Jewish women by the sermonizer Jacob Ben Yitshak Ashkenazi at the end of the sixteenth century), which she had carried with her all the way from Krasnocielc. In order to strengthen our spirits, she told us stories and folk tales from the book. We liked to hear the following tale:

> In the time of Rabbi Akiva, the Romans prohibited the Jewish people from studying the Torah. Rabbi Akiva's disciples came to him and asked him, "How can we stop studying the Torah?" Rabbi Akiva answered them with an allegory: "One day the cunning fox came to the river. He saw the fish running all over the place and wished to eat them. He told them: 'Fish, fish, why are you purposelessly wandering around like that? It would be better for you to come out here to the land, warm yourselves up under the rays of the shining sun and find peace for your souls.' The head fish answered him: 'Fox, indeed here there are many dangers threatening us and we run all over the place in order to avoid them, but we at least are in our natural environment. If we go out to land and leave our natural environment, it will be difficult for us to cope with our problems. The sun will dry us up or you will eat us.'" Rabbi Akiva added that the allegory referred to the people of Israel, who may be in danger while studying the Torah, but at least they are in their natural habitat. If they stopped studying the Torah, they would face the danger of extinction.

In October 1940, Moshe and Aharon were transferred to work in the village of Wietki, located nine miles from Kiltowo. There, too, they engaged in tree-related jobs, but conditions were even harsher. Every Saturday night they walked back to Kiltowo to help us with heating the house and on Mondays they returned to Wietki.

In May 1941, Aharon joined a group engaged in marking the Kiltowo woods. He had to walk through the woods and mark trees that were as high as people with his axe so that in the winter the woodchoppers would be able to identify the trees for cutting. One morning Aharon went out to work as usual with a group of about fifteen people. At a certain point, the Russian foreman asked him to look for the person who carried the berry bucket and replace him in that job. Aharon left to look for that man, but could not find him. After searching for about half an hour, he became afraid of getting lost – a common phenomenon in those woods. He started to cry out for his friends, pleading with them to shout back at him so that he could return to them. But because Aharon would often trick his friends in this way, they thought that he was joking again and decided to ignore his calls. Aharon stayed alone in the woods, worried and fearful, trying to find a way out. He walked for many hours until he arrived at the village of Vielordim during the afternoon hours of the next day. There he met an acquaintance from his former workplace and told him about his situation. The acquaintance hurried to call Kiltowo to let them know that Aharon was alive. We family members exhaled with relief. We had been afraid that Aharon had lost his way in the taiga, as only a few people survived after wandering around all night long. The next morning Aharon started to walk toward Kiltowo, but on the way he was stopped by NKVD officers who found it hard to believe his story. He was taken to an investigation office in the neighboring town and was released only after they found a witness who confirmed his story.

In the summer of 1941 Aharon and Moshe were sent to Wietki again, where they worked for four months in preparing hay before the coming of winter. They lived in tents, could not wash themselves and worked under very hard conditions. Bad sores developed on their skins which did not heal for many days.

During that period we continued to correspond with my brother Yosef in Palestine, and even received packages from him through the American Jewish Joint Distribution Committee and other rescue organizations. We corresponded also with my brother Hershel who had remained in Bialystok. He sent us packages with necessities – soap, sugar and some flour. In one of his letters Hershel said that he wanted to join us. My mother replied that he would be better off in Bialystok, and he would be better able to help us from afar. In later years, my mother suffered keenly from this reply. She believed that if he had joined us he might have stayed alive.

In the summer of 1941 we stopped receiving letters from Hershel. Only many years later we found out that he had been summoned by the Russians to defend a fortress located on the Bug River. The Germans who conquered the region murdered all the Communists and Jews who were among the captives. An eyewitness told me that Hershel had been one of them.

The information about his death shocked me very much. Hershel, my dear brother who believed in socialism, who had made it possible for me to look for the first time beyond my narrow Jewish experience and see something of the world outside; Hershel, who had told us to cut our side locks, replace our traditional clothes and go out to support ourselves; Hershel, who had investigated the circumstances of father's death, while all of us prayed for his memory. The initial reservations that I had had as a child of his "different" way turned in the course of years into an unbounded admiration – an admiration for a person who thought for himself, for a person who was at once both an idealist and a pragmatic. Many years later, we called our youngest son after him, Lior-Zvi.

In June 1941, after the German invasion of the USSR, the exiled government of Poland in London, headed by General Shikorsky, reached an agreement with Stalin on a number of issues. First and foremost, the Poles agreed to establish a Polish army which would fight the Germans together with the Red Army (in later years this organization was called the Anders Army). At the same time, the Soviets agreed to improve the conditions of Polish citizens who were refugees in the USSR. They also consented to grant Polish education to the children from Poland, a decision from which I could also benefit.

After the agreement was made all Jewish and Polish residents in Kiltowo were summoned to a meeting, where we were informed that from that day on we could go anywhere in Russia without any restrictions. In the beginning of September and after a family consultation, Aharon and Bronia left Kiltowo for Komi's capital, Siktivkar, to look for a job and a residence for us all. At that time tens of thousands of men who were released from prisoner camps were also seeking jobs in Siktivkar, but Bronia and Aharon succeeded in finding jobs supplying wood to heat the town's public institutions. Every day they sailed on a raft on a broad and turbulent river and gathered wood for heating. They found an apartment for us in the Ciencikowa neighborhood, which had rows of identical wooden homes. Each row had ten apartments, and Aharon and Bronia happily informed us that they found an apartment in the "fifth group of ten." In September 1941 we traveled to Siktivkar in trucks and joined the two.

In those days, we considered leaving the Komi region and moving to the Tashkent region in central Asia, but we could get there by boat only as long as the river was not frozen. Since at this time both Aharon and Mother became ill and were admitted to hospitals in town, we had to postpone the idea of leaving. Aharon still suffered from the sores he had developed in Wietki and Mother's health was deteriorating so we stayed in Siktivkar and tried to support ourselves. The food was allotted with coupons. Each person received coupons for two days – six hundred grams of bread for working people and four hundred grams for "dependent" people, such as the elderly, children and the sick. After mother was released from the hospital, she collected the bread and every day, at dawn, divided it into portions. None of us objected to the size of the bread allotted to him, but in other homes the distribution of bread caused nasty arguments and sometimes even fights. We accepted Mother's decisions then as well as during the entire journey without any dispute. Moshe, who did not have to work most of the time because of the weakness he had from the typhoid he suffered used to go to town and trade with food coupons. He sold tomorrow's bread for today's soup and was happy when he could obtain a portion of bread or soup with these tricks. Later on he was assigned to a job of weaving baskets from branches. The Polish *poselstwo* (consulate) which operated in the USSR obtained light jobs for the handicapped. After Aharon was released from the hospital he started to work at different jobs. Among others, he worked as a hog herder in a Sovchoz, a national agricultural farm out of town, which was ran by a Jew called Orbach, who employed Jews under relatively good conditions. Leah worked for the local NKVD commander since she had picked up Russian rather quickly.

Because of the ever-present danger of epidemics, disinfections were carried out from time to time. We were stopped by policemen in the street without any prior warning and taken in a truck to the regional public bathhouse. There we were undressed and our clothes were taken from us to be disinfected in a hot-water boiler. In the meantime we were sprayed with DDT and only after all of this were we released.

Generally, the conditions in Siktivkar were better than in Kiltowo. If we had the money, we could buy products in the town's shops and we were allowed to practice Judaism. In Passover of the year 1942, my mother decided to observe the kashrut laws of the holiday. She gave us her portion of bread and ate only potatoes during the holiday, which she had saved for herself during the preceding months.

One day Yitshak showed me a loaf of bread that he pulled out of his pocket. The person responsible for distributing the food had probably made a mistake and given him more than his allotment; we celebrated the rare occasion. He shared the loaf of bread with me and later also with the rest of the family.

During that period I had the opportunity of contributing my own share to support the family. One day while I was walking in town, a policeman stopped me and accused me of vagrancy. He brought me to the police station and ordered me to report to the chief, who asked me who I was. I told him my name and explained to him that I was a Jewish boy from Poland. He ordered his men to find out if the details I gave him were correct and in the meantime asked me if I happened to know how to play chess. I told him yes, whereupon he led me to his private room and pulled out a chess board and wooden soldiers from one of the drawers and we started to play. After a short time I won the game. The chief was impressed with the way I played and invited me to play with him again. He explained that he liked chess very much, but unfortunately he didn't have a worthy partner. He wrapped half a loaf of bread in a newspaper and gave it to me. "Every time you come here," he said, "I will give you such a gift, because I would like you to come here out of your own free will." I was very happy as half a loaf of bread was a serious addition to the family's nutrition. And so, every week, I went back to the chief's office and played chess with him. Sometimes I won and other times he won, but in either case he gave me the half a loaf of bread and the whole family enjoyed it throughout the week. The chief also gave me a note saying he knew me personally and that I should be allowed to walk freely in the town. Unfortunately, the successful arrangement ended a few months later once he was transferred elsewhere.

During the summer vacation all the children in the Komi region were recruited for different jobs. I was sent to a government farm that grew hogs. In the farm I was responsible for making sure that the hogs didn't run away and to catch them if they tried. In the beginning I was disgusted by the idea of being in contact with the hogs, as Jewish law forbids eating them, but gradually, thanks to my mother's encouragement, I adapted to the situation. As payment for my work I received food coupons with which we purchased food at the local store.

Sometimes I was also employed in picking potatoes in a government kolkhoz. Healthy, strong women worked with me and showed their patriotism by singing nationalist songs while they worked. With us also worked a tractor driver, whose job was to overturn the earth near the potato shrubs. One day I noticed that the tractor driver dug only every second row, so that the clods of earth covered the seeding in the rows he skipped. This way half the crop was buried instead of being picked. That day we ended our work around one o'clock in the afternoon since we had met our daily quota earlier than usual. We were praised by our supervisors. We then decided to go back to the field in the afternoon where we picked up the potatoes which were intentionally left and divided them among ourselves. The adults received full bags but I, as a child, received only a few potatoes. I was still glad as it was also better than nothing. Every help I could give my family contributed to our support, and especially to my self-esteem.

One day in the summer of 1942 Moshe was arrested by the police. The reason was falling behind in work. The policemen came to our house searching for evidence against him, and found a card which proved him to be active in the past in the Hapoel Hamizrachi movement. The card was taken and the police used it to blame Moshe for treason, which worsened conditions of his imprisonment. We never heard from him again. Later we found out that he had died in prison, probably as a result of a heart attack due to the harsh conditions. I called my second son Noam Moshe in his memory.

In late August we were ordered to move to a place called Pezmog in the county of Korkiruz. There was a large wood factory there. Immediately upon our arrival the four youngest children – Yitshak, Malka, Elimelech and I, were taken to a children's house in the village of Dodj. The place lay about fifteen miles from Siktivkar. Pezmog was considered an exile within an exile; only working adults were to stay there.

Bronia had been away from us when we were ordered by the authorities to move to Pezmog. When she found out about our "exile," she was able to make contact with a Jewish family living in Siktivkar by the name of Shidlo. In exchange for assisting them with their small children, she was permitted to live at their place. With supreme effort she succeeded in enabling the adults in Pezmog – Mother, Aharon and Leah – to move back to Siktivkar one by one and join her in Shidlo's cramped house. At the time these successful efforts were considered life saving, since coping with the harsh conditions in Pezmog – hard labor, extreme cold and famine – were beyond human endurance. Mother, Aharon and Leah witnessed people dying in front of them more than once.

Once Yitshak and I had the opportunity and decided to visit our mother in Pezmog. We had to walk fifteen miles in snow that came up to our waist – but we made it to Mother.

Living in the children's house in the village of Dodj was also trying. There was no school. Six children slept in each room. Every morning we had to make our beds and meet the schedule set by the people who ran the place. If someone did not meet this schedule, he was punished "for his own good" and was sent to wash dishes, clean house or work shifts in the dining room.

The food in the children's house was allotted and the portions were very small, so we never felt satisfied. We were hungry all the time and did not meticulously examine the food which was served, which probably caused us to eat non-kosher meat. One day, some of the Polish children who lived in the children's house, out of great hunger, killed a dog and ate its meat. The staff in the place considered it a serious offense not because dog meat was unfit for human consumption, but because it was a guard dog and the act was seen as damaging government property. They tried us collectively, and we were punished.

Another trauma that I remember from the children's house is related to the death of a roommate, a Polish boy named Karol. He became ill with tuberculosis and coughed and spit blood for a long time. After he died, a coffin was brought to our room, and his body was placed in it. As was customary with Christians, the coffin remained for a few days in the room. One night I was horrified to notice that the cover on the coffin was rising by itself. I was overwhelmed with fear. I was trembling and could not calm down. Later on it became clear to me that the bloating corpse was pushing the coffin's cover up.

As part of the agreement between the Russian government and the Polish exiled government, the Russians agreed to establish a model Polish school. Their object was to preserve Polish culture and create a new generation of Polish intelligentia. The school was established in the town of Zagorsk, near Moscow. Ms. Benzon, who was chosen to run the school, gathered talented children for her school from all over the country. I was also chosen, the only one from among the students in Kirpichney Zavod, the children's home that I transferred to in order to be close to my family.

One day, toward the end of the summer of 1943, a police officer came to take me to the new school. My mother was very sad when she heard the news. She was afraid that my fate would be like those Jewish boys, the Cantonists, who were kidnapped to serve in the Russian army during the days of the czar and there underwent conversion and were never heard from again. I tried to cheer her up and promised that I would write, but she cried a lot and refused to be comforted. Yet, as always, when the order came from the authorities it had to be obeyed. I sailed with the officer by boat to the town of Kotlas. From there we continued by train to Zagorsk, which was located at a distance of fifteen hundred miles from Siktivkar.

In the autumn of 1943, at the age of thirteen, I started to study in the school in Zagorsk.

I was totally cut off from my family. About thirty boys and girls participated in the class. Apart from a small number of Jewish children, most students were children of the Polish bourgeois and men of the Catholic religion who had been deported in 1939 from the German region after Poland was divided between Russia and Germany. In time, we were joined by more children who were war orphans or whose parents had good connections and wanted their children to study at this highly prestigious school.

We studied many subjects, among them history, geography, Polish, English, mathematics, writing and drawing. Most lessons were held in Polish, except history and Russian literature and linguistics which were held in Russian. Most teachers were Polish and I remember with pleasure the class's homeroom teacher, Ms. Penzonowa. She taught history and literature and had a wide range of knowledge. Apart from direct teaching, she also guided our class and exposed me to the elite authors of world literature. In my eyes, the eyes of a young boy eager to quench his thirst for knowledge, Ms. Penzonowa seemed a real intellectual power. I had always loved to study, and here, too, I quickly adapted to studying and was considered an exemplary student. I won books as prizes for excellence a few times, as a result of which I was appointed to be the editor of the school's newspaper. I also had the opportunity of playing chess again in the new school, and it did not take me long to be considered the school's best chess player.

My excellence in studies did not harm my social life in school. I was popular and appreciated by my friends, mainly because I often helped them in their studies. Once in a while I faced acts of anti-Semitism, especially from children new to the school since the prejudices against Jews were rooted deeply in them. In such cases I used to talk to them in all seriousness and explain like an adult that "ignorance is the greatest foe of mankind." The teachers were satisfied by my involvement and claimed that with my personality, I helped them educate others.

At school I had a few close friends. Two of them, Edward Wiszniewski and Boleslaw Malc, were especially close to me and we often discussed politics and religion and played games together. I also had two female friends. The first was Frieda, a pretty and intelligent Jewish girl with whom I used to hold long conversations. To my other female friend, a Polish girl named Marisia who was more down to earth, I was mainly attracted physically. We both were shy and naive and we did not go further than holding hands – and even this was done discretely so as not to create gossip.

The school's living conditions were very good. There were twelve children in each room, and each was given a single bed and a small bookcase. Every morning we rose at seven o'clock, exercised for fifteen minutes, put on our black-and-white uniform and headed toward the dining room for a light breakfast. The studies went on until four o'clock in the afternoon, during which we had a half-hour lunch break. After four o'clock we spent time with each other, reading, listening to classical music, playing chess or billiards and participating in various courses, such as ballroom dancing and singing in the choir. I sang in the school's choir. Around seven thirty we had supper, which was the main meal of the day and occasionally included meat or fish. Around nine o'clock the lights went off.

The quantity of food we were given in school was reasonable, but as typical of young adolescents, we were often hungry. The school's Polish cook liked me, probably because I excelled in my studies, and hinted that I could return to her and receive a second portion. I usually avoided doing so because I was afraid of evoking the jealousy of the other children.

Once in a while we had activities outside the school grounds. Sometimes they took us on tours and trips to the beautiful town of Zagorsk and other times they showed us boring propaganda films of the Communist regime. One day I couldn't stand the boredom and left the movie theater. Our homeroom teacher hurried after me and threatened that if I did that again, I would be expelled from school.

We traveled to Moscow a few times by trolley. During the first visit we watched the play *The Mother* by Gorki and afterwards ate ice cream, which was kept outside the freezer since the natural cold kept it frozen. Moscow seemed a magical and very beautiful city. The visit excited me and I remember thinking that this was how the capital of the Russian people had to look like.

On the eve of January 1, 1944, we were invited to take part in a festive reception to welcome the New Year in *Dom Soyuzow*, the house of the Soviet people's Board of Laborers. *Dom Soyuzow* was a large and impressive building – one of Moscow's most magnificent buildings in those days. The building was decorated with the dolls of "Uncle Frost," the secular figures that became old Santa Claus's substitute in the atheist Soviet culture. An evergreen tree with beautiful ornaments was standing inside the building and colorful gifts were placed around it. The sounds of pleasant music came from all the rooms in the building. I felt like Alice in Wonderland. At the reception ceremony, I was presented as the best student of the school by Wanda Wasilewska, a famous author who wrote the anti-Nazi book *The Rainbow in the Cloud* and served as the chairman of the Exiled Polish Patriots Association to which the school in Zagorsk belonged. In the course of the ceremony I was honored to shake hands with the "generalissimo" – that was how she introduced the man – Joseph Vissarionovich Stalin. And thus I, little David Himmelfarb, stood before the legendary "Sun of All Nations," Stalin the Great, the ruler of the USSR, and shook his hands. For me, it was an exhilarating moment, full of great enthusiasm.

Invitation to the Kremlin
With the New Year
"Uncle Frost" has given us instructions
to invite you to the Hall of Columns (in the Kremlin)
A. 108528, November 20, 1944

It is no wonder then that the period of my studies in Zagorsk served as both an intellectual and an ideological springboard for me. There I was exposed to the great writers of world literature – Russian authors, such as Gorki,

Dostoyevsky, Pushkin, Lermontov and Tolstoy; English authors, such as Dickens and Sir Arthur Conan Doyle; and Polish authors such as Sienkiewicz, Mickiewicz and Wasilewska. In addition, I became familiar with books related to the field of military history. I read a lot about the French Revolution, about the Polish wars of independence and about the revolutions and wars in Russia. I was mainly touched by Tolstoy's words in his book *War and Peace*.

Yet my ideological outlook also went through a thorough shake-up. Like all my friends, I, too, underwent Soviet indoctrination. We had many newspapers at school and I eagerly read them. Almost all newspapers – Polish, Russian and English – contained virulent propaganda articles against the Germans and news of mass murders committed by them in Russian towns (news about extermination camps had not yet been published). When the news of the Warsaw Ghetto Uprising was published, I was proud to be Jewish. In addition, I identified with the struggle of the Jewish people against the British in Palestine. I considered the Russians natural allies of the Jewish people in their fight against the common German foe. I appreciated their contribution very much and was aware of their many sacrifices. The Soviet Army lost about nine to ten million male and female soldiers during their war against the Nazis. Among these about 250,000 were Jewish soldiers. I was proud when I found out that many great revolutionaries, such as Marx, Trotsky and Kaganovitz were Jewish. Gradually a new identity started to form in me. The Hasidic passiveness I was brought up on slowly gave way to a strong aspiration for freedom and a willingness to fight for my rights. I understood that my personal struggle was also public. It was in those days that the principles of social and political involvement, which I acted on years later in Israel, were inculcated in me.

During the first months of my studies at school, I practiced Judaism as much as I could. Every morning I woke up early and went up in the cold to the attic, where I quickly prayed. I hid because I was afraid of being caught praying. But as time went by cracks started to appear in my religious beliefs and I gradually discontinued practicing Judaism. The change was mainly due to the communist education I received, which saw religion as "opium for the masses," but the "blame" must not be put only on it. I started to have doubts and questions which remained unanswered. I was alone not only in the physical sense, far from my family members and their influence, but also in the spiritual sense. I asked myself how the intelligent Jewish people could for generations lock themselves up against all external influences. I tried to talk about it with some of my teachers and friends, but I could not share these thoughts with my family – not only because of the geographic distance.

I was overwhelmed by ambivalent feelings. On the one hand, I felt that I had gradually distanced myself from my family and from my old world, and on the other hand, I missed my mother very much. It was that distance that made me appreciate her practicality and her daily struggle against the hardships of life even more. My mother had always been an active woman who fought for herself and her family, and these attributes were expressed even more during the times in which fate forced her to function as the head of the family. Paradoxically, I found that my mother's values actually corresponded with my new ones – values of action, performance and struggle. Again and again I was overwhelmed with feelings of longing mixed with a sense of guilt, pain and confusion.

I continued corresponding with my mother in Yiddish. The letters were transferred in various and strange ways: by boats which sailed on the rivers, on trucks and so on, and sometimes two to three weeks went by until they reached their destination. In these letters I mainly reported to her about my academic success in school, but I did not tell her anything about changes in my outlook. The fact that I wrote my mother in Yiddish, in Hebrew letters, from right to left, evoked the attention of my Polish friends, who occasionally harassed me with irritating questions, such as whether the orders to murder Jesus were written in this language. I wanted to avoid these insults, and therefore preferred to write to her in a hiding place. During that period I also started to "degrade" the Yiddish language, seeing it as a language fit for jokes and small talk, but inferior to the "classic" languages.

At the end of 1943, representatives of the Polish army came to our school and asked us to join the army's youth battalions. Back then my feelings were very patriotic and I was passionate to revenge myself on the Germans, and decided to volunteer. My favorite song at the time was "*Leningrad ne sdadim, ne stariju stolizu Ladogu perejdiom, vstaniom na granice* (Leningrad will not surrender. It is our ancient capital. We will cross the Ladoga and return to our border)."

I also wanted to show to all the anti-Semites that Jews could fight exactly like Gentiles. Six to seven other boys from school also volunteered, and another Jewish boy, named Sewek, was among them.

I presented my decision to join the youth battalions to my mother as an accomplished fact. Later on I found out that she objected, fearing that I would share the fate of the Cantonists.

The Polish army representatives asked the school's management to recommend us, the volunteers. But they also interviewed us in order to check the extent of our patriotism. Afterwards they trained us for a few days. These trainings included field trainings, gymnastics and ice skating. Apart from that, they taught us to play wind instruments so that we could take part in a band that played at the head of military parades.

I was very emotional on my departure from my teachers and friends in school. I will never forget my homeroom teacher telling me: "You are now about to turn from an adolescent into an adult." I knew that I would miss my friends and the atmosphere at school. In spite of my young age, I understood that it was an important period in my life, which contributed greatly to my personal development and to the person that I am today.

In the beginning of the year 1944, I left school in Zagorsk and was transferred to an academy that trained Polish army officers in the town of Riazan near Moscow. In this academy, thousands of eighteen-year-old male and female cadets took part in an exhausting officers' course which lasted a few months. There were many Russians and Polish ex-farmers and Yiddish-speaking Jews. The small number of showers in the camp forced the commanders to send us, the boys, to shower with female combat cadets and nurses. We were very embarrassed when we met them through the clouds of steam.

I belonged to the youth company at the officers' academy. The company consisted of about forty Polish boys, aged thirteen to sixteen. Three of them were Jewish. Our company was called the Eagle's Cubs, as the eagle was the symbol of the Polish army.

In the school in Riazan we had different classes such as gunnery, communication, ski, riding, using weapons, military history and communist education. A number of hours were also designated every day for general studies such as mathematics, history and physics. As in Zagorsk, in Riazan I was also considered one of the best students. We also learned how to play various instruments and our music accompanied the officers' graduation ceremonies as we marched in front of the row of cadets. I blew a large alto trumpet. Occasionally we had to run in the trenches in order to pass on information.

As the communication lines in the front were often cut off, cadets served as messengers who had to transfer information from one unit to the other.

In the military academy discipline was very strict. Every morning we woke up early and put on our uniforms. Our berets and boots had to be polished daily until they shone "like a mirror." After the short morning exercise, washup and breakfast, we were engaged all day long in studies, training and homework until the late hours of the night.

In general, I enjoyed the period of studies in the military academy. I had a place to live and the food was fine. I was an excellent student and my friends loved me. I also did not have any problems with the physical training. I dreamed of completing the course, leaving for battle and receiving a medal for an act of courage. This wish was the result of much indoctrination about the importance of self-sacrifice and of causing the enemy as much damage as possible. I was also influenced back in those days from the book *The People of Panpilov* and its characters, a group of Soviet soldiers who sacrificed their lives in the defense of Moscow. This book also inspired the fighters of the Palmach. In addition, I was influenced by pictures of heroism displayed on the walls of the camp's entertainment hall, which usually presented injured and bleeding heroes.

One day the sergeant informed me that the commander wished to see me. My heart beat fast as I was afraid that something horrible was about to happen to me. When I arrived in his room, the commander ordered the sergeant to leave the room. Then he approached me and said, "Take a paper and a pencil and write down: Rosh Hashanah falls on ___ and Yom Kippur falls on ___ (he named their respective dates). Does this tell you anything?" I answered, "Yes, I was brought up in a religious home." I was afraid to tell him that I was religious. Then the commander ordered me: "Go back to your duty, turn back!" and rang the bell so that the sergeant would come back and escort me outside. I found this event to be very strange and tried for years to understand the meaning of the officer's behavior. The only explanation I could figure out was that the commander was probably Jewish himself, and in his act he wished to remind me of my origin and of the principles of the Jewish tradition which I was gradually forgetting.

Back in Siktivkar, my family continued to persevere. Aharon tried his luck at a number of places of work – first as a fire stoker in an institution, and later in a garage. After a while he found a job clearing off wooden beams that were cut down in the winter and moving them to float in the river, which was a dangerous job but a relatively profitable one. In October 1943, he started to work at a wood plant in Siktivkar called Les Zawod, but after arriving late a few times – the penalty for which was a prison sentence – he decided to run away from the plant in the spring of 1944. He did so, and reached the railway station in Knieszpogost from which he traveled toward Kotlas. During a strict inspection that was carried out in the train, Aharon was caught without documents and brought in a prisoners train back to Knieszpogost, where he was arrested. Afterwards he was forced to walk one hundred fifty kilometers (ninety-five miles) to Siktivkar. The journey weakened him very much and upon his arrival in Komi, he asked permission to call Bronia and then lost consciousness. Thanks to Bronia's treatment his life was saved. At this stage he was tried for trying to run away and the judge, an eighteen-year-old youth, sentenced him to four months in the Wierchnichov labor camp, where he was lucky to be hospitalized for two weeks thanks to a note written by Dr. Spielman. During these two weeks he recovered from his exhaustion.

One day Aharon came to visit me in Riazan. I was very surprised as he arrived there by mistake. He made his way to Ukraine and stopped in Moscow, went to take a walk in town and missed the train. He was left without documents, money or clothes. One way or another he succeeded in boarding another train, and as he did not have money for the ticket, he climbed onto the locomotive. During the ride he was arrested by guards, but after begging and pleading he succeeded in convincing them that he was not a criminal. When he arrived at the outskirts of the city of Riazan, he remembered that I stayed there. When I first saw him, he seemed miserable and said that he was very hungry. I managed to find a piece of bread for him, which he eagerly swallowed. Unfortunately, he was prohibited from staying in the military camp and was forced to continue his journey, but he felt better because of the rest, and the small amount of food that he had put in his mouth made him feel as if he had reached heaven. Many years later he told me that that piece of bread saved his life.

My brother Yitshak studied in the vocational school at FZO, and in the summer of 1943 he was sent to work in a *splaw* (raft), navigating bundles of wooden logs down the river. With the help of a long, wooden spear, he had to prevent the logs from hitting the riverbank. The *splaw* was considered very dangerous work because one could slip from the logs into very cold water. Yitshak told us that one day, while he tried to reach the riverbank to get out of the water, he found that the section of the river that was adjacent to the riverbank had frozen and the layer of ice covering the water was too thin to walk on. He was unable to climb to the riverbank. Fortunately a boat with people equipped with axes sailed by. They broke the ice – difficult and dangerous work in its own right – and only after long, fear-filled hours was he eventually able to climb to the riverbank. Another time his finger got stuck between two wooden beams and broke.

In the summer of 1944, as a result of the Russian army's progress westward, a general amnesty was declared for all of Poland's citizens, which allowed my family to leave the Komi region and come close to the Russian-Polish border. My family boarded river boats and sailed to Ukraine. On the way, so they told me, they sang the song "Goodbye, Goodbye" over and over again in Russian. A short while after the Germans were driven out of the area, my family arrived in the village of Wolfino in Kursk Region, Ukraine. Each family was given a room, and everyone started to work in the local kolkhozes. The life in Wolfino was considered a real improvement compared to the period they spent in European Siberia, as they at last had the luxury of tasting eggs, milk and onions, which they had not even dared dream of before.

During that period I was glad to receive letters from them, in which they begged me to join them. At the same time they sent my military commanders requests to release me. Bronia even made three risky visits to Moscow in order to intercede with the authorities, arguing that my mother was sick and that she urgently needed my help. And indeed, one day in the year 1945, after I had served for two years in the youth battalions of the military academy, my commander suddenly called me and told me to join the rest of my family to help them. I packed my belongings and traveled to Zagorsk. There I met my sister Bronia, and together we traveled to Wolfino. After being apart from them for a period of two and a half years, I finally joined my beloved family.

I was very glad to be reunited with my family, but the transition from life in the military academy to life in a shack where the whole family lived was not simple. It was a transition from a comfortable life to a daily existential struggle; from an environment where I received attention and appreciation to one where my achievements were insignificant; from an atmosphere that nurtured collective ideology and glorified dreams and actions to one of asceticism and separatism; and mainly, from a lifestyle of absolute secularity to one of strict religiosity. I felt like a swan forced to fall back on a flock of ducks. I was not very close to my siblings, and my relationship with my mother was fraught with tension. Every time I tried to talk to her and describe to her the other lifestyle I had experienced and its advantages, she tried to convince me that I had been influenced by a lie. I became increasingly frustrated and began to hold grudges against her, but I had no way to express my feelings. I succeeded in hiding my distress from the others, but at night I would cry into my pillows.

A short time after my arrival to Wolfino, I started to study in the regional school which was located in Tiotkino, about four miles from the village. One day on the way to school, Yitshak and I were harassed by two Gentile boys who took my ski poles from me. Without the poles I could not progress in the snow, and I felt helpless and angry. Eventually, I rescued myself with a branch I found. I managed quite well in my studies, although I had to get used to the Russian language again, since at Zagorsk and Riazan I had studied mainly in Polish.

In April 1945 I moved with Yitshak and Malka to the village of Tiotkino. Bronia and Leah remained in Wolfino and started to work in the village sugar factory, while Elimelech attended school there. His teachers soon found him to be an excellent student, and his friends even called him "*Mali Lenin* (Little Lenin)." We studied in Tiotkino only for a short while, and during the summer vacation I was assigned to various jobs in the village of Wolfino, such as picking vegetables and cleaning the fields.

In the meantime, in the beginning of 1945 Aharon was recruited into the Russian army and later to the Polish army. In March 1945 his unit assisted at the liberated Majdanek extermination camp near Lublin, and afterwards he moved to a military camp in Lodz, where he stayed until Germany's final surrender in May 1945.

Throughout our years of wandering in Russia we were usually freezing and stricken with hunger but we managed to survive, if only through our utmost efforts. At that time we had no idea that six million Jewish people were being murdered in the Holocaust. Thirty-three hundred thousand of the victims were from Poland. As far as I could find out, my paternal grandfather and maternal grandmother as well as my uncles, aunts and their children were all exterminated by the Germans in Treblinka. Unfortunately, neither I nor my brothers could discover any details about our relatives' last journey.

Medals and Tokens

Several of the tokens and medals that David Himmelfarb received which respect the chronology of events in his life.

Left to right:
1. Memorial pin for Holocaust survivors – Yad Vashem
2. Marshal Zhukov Medal – for participation in World War II
3. Gold Medal of the Polish Army – for service in the Polish army
4. Token of the Palmach and Machal – for volunteering for service in the Independence War 1948
5. Knight's Cross – for service to the Polish Republic (establishment of memorials at Krasnosielc Poland and on Mount Herzl, Jerusalem)

Gabriel Missile Project: the missile boat in a position to launch the missile

With pilot Mario Barcini, general manager of Europa Airlines, at the Aviation Exhibition in Paris, 1983

Chaya and David at the Piazza Navona in Rome, 1973

Aharon, David's brother, saying Kaddish
by the common grave at the memorial site at Krasnosielc, Poland

A delegation of children from Kibbutz Tirat Tzvi at the Krasnosielc memorial site

From right to left: Mr. Sami Shamoon, among the main donors for establishing the memorial on Mount Herzl; David; the Polish military attaché Brigadier General Edward Kucharski and his adjutant Major Grezegorz Blaszcyk

The chaplain of the Anders Army, Rabbi Pinchas Rozengartin, and the military attaché, Edward Kucharski, at the foot of the memorial in Jerusalem, with representatives of the Polish army

Officer of the Polish army places a wreath at the foot of the memorial.

With Polish soldiers from the Polish UN unit (Polbatt) in the Golan. On the left is Mr. Uri Navon, head of the Mount Herzl Military Cemetary.

The memorial on Mount Herzl dedicated to the memory of fallen Jewish soldiers who served in the Polish armies between the years 1939–1945

David speaking at the inauguration of the memorial in Jerusalem, 1998.
In the background is an inscription in Polish: "To our freedom and your freedom."

David speaking on the anniversary of the establishment of the memorial in Jerusalem; in the background, the words in Polish: "For Our Freedom, and for Your Freedom"

A visit by the prime minister of Poland, Mr. Alexander Kwasniewski, at the memorial

At the founding meeting for the establishment of the Jewish Museum in Warsaw, 2001, with Mr. Sami Shamoon, his wife Angela and Lord Ganer, a member of the British Parliament

Mr. Sami Shamoon with a medal from the Polish government for his contributions to the Republic of Poland

Plaque in honor of donors for the establishment of the monument on Mount Herzl: Mr. Sami Shamoon and Yosef Maimon and family (see appendix for text)

The Himmelfarb Family before the outbreak of World War II

A map of the location of Krasnosielc in the Mazovia Province, Poland (Hebrew)

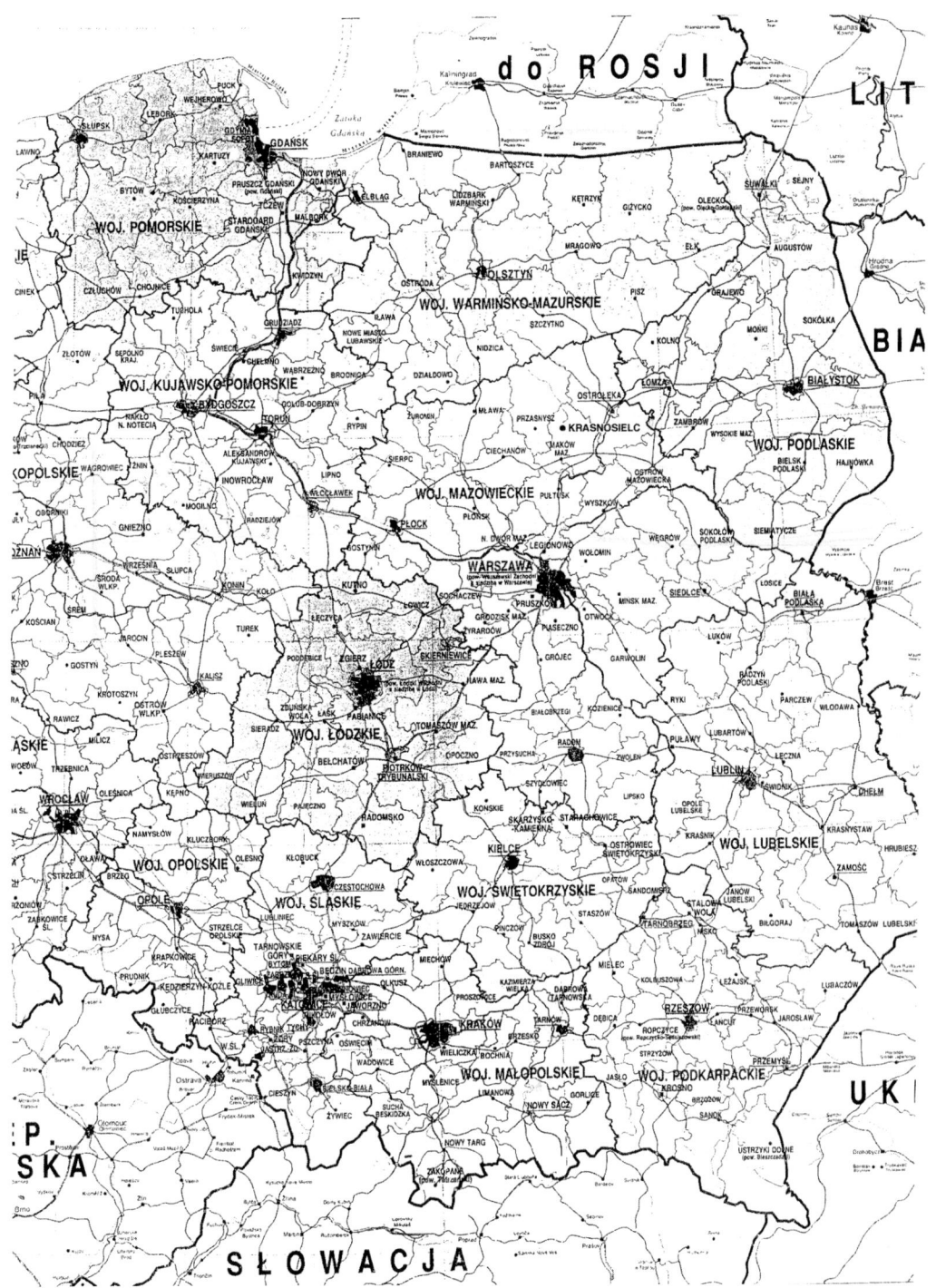

A map of the location of Krasnosielc in the Mazovia Province, Poland (Polish)

The synagogue of the town of Krasnosielc

A roundup of Jews in the neighboring town of Govorovo

A group of Jews from the town of Krasnosielc, 1929.
Among them Dr. Spielman, who cared for David's mother and family in Siberia.

The French Commando at the successful conquest of Tamila Command Post,
December 1948

David in the model school for Polish children
in the town of Zagorsk (near Moscow), 1943

In a winter uniform of the Polish army, Riazan, 1944
(*third from left*)

The first marriage in the family since the shoah:
David's sister Bronia and her husband Rabbi Issac Goralnik, 1946

David in the Palmach, 1948

David in the Polish army, 1944 (*first on left*)

At the museum of Kibbutz Nirim with the mortar used in Operation Horeb
(Capture of Beer Sheva)

David at the memorial for the Machal fallen, 1948.
In the background is the dedication of Prime Minister Yitzhak Rabin.

Last photo with "French suit" in the streets of Haifa, 1949

With the training team of the electronic company at the Navy Training Base, 1954

David and Chaya at their marriage, Haifa 1954

Organization of a soccer game between Kiryat Shmona
and a team of kibbutzim in the vicinity, in the framework of the Rotary Club, 1964

David and Chaya's three children at Kibbutz Kfar Blum, 1966

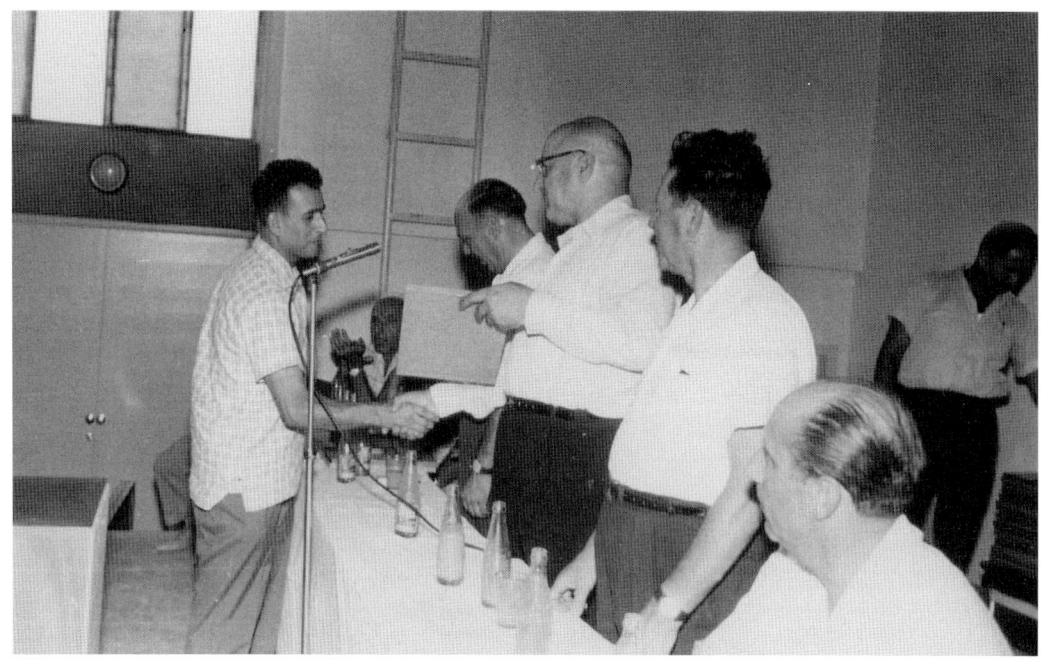

Pinchas Sapir, minister of commerce and industry,
gives David a medal of esteem for his activities in Kiryat Shmona, 1964.

A farewell party at the Mabat Company of the Israeli Aircraft Corporation
before David commenced his new position as representative of Mabat in Italy

David at a reception for Prime Minister Ariel Sharon, 2003

David with his friend, the Polish writer and journalist Marian Bondarchuk, 1995

The cultural attaché Doctor Suzanne Reiner of the German Embassy in Israel signs the Golden Book of the Keren Kayemet of Israel.

At the establishment of the memorial site at Krasnosielc, 1996

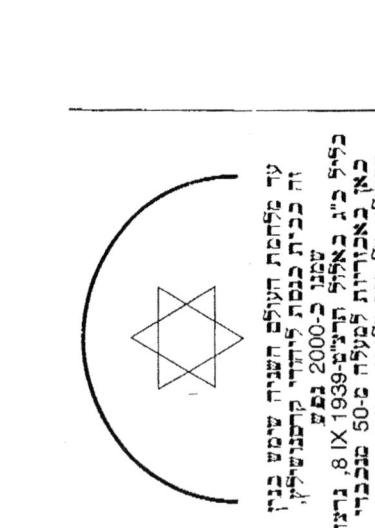

THIS BUILDING WAS THE SYNA-
GOGUE OF 2000 MEMBERS OF THE
JEWISH COMMUNITY OF KRASNO-
SIELC, UNTIL WORLD WAR II.
HERE ON THE NIGHT OF 8 IX 1939
MORE THAN 50 PROMINENT MEM-
BERS OF THE COMMUNITY WERE
BRUTALLY MURDERED BY THE
NAZI-GERMANS AND THEIR BODIES
BURIED IN THE ADJOINING YARD.
THE REMAINDER OF THE COM-
MUNITY WAS THEN DRIVEN OUT
THROUGH ACTS OF TERROR TO
A BITTER FATE.

ASSOCIATION OF FORMER
KRASNOSIELC RESIDENTS
IN ISRAEL AND U.S.A. 1996

W TYM BUDYNKU DO POCZĄTKU
II WOJNY ŚWIATOWEJ MIEŚ-
CIŁA SIĘ SYNAGOGA GMINNA
2000 ŻYDÓW KRASNOSIELCA.
TU W NOCY 8 IX 1939 ROKU
HITLEROWCY BRUTALNIE ZAMOR-
DOWALI PONAD 50 ZASŁUŻONYCH
CZŁONKÓW MIEJSCOWEJ GMINY.
ICH CIAŁA POCHOWANO NA
PRZYLEGŁYM PODWÓRZU.
WKRÓTCE POTEM POZOSTAŁA
CZĘŚĆ SPOŁECZNOŚCI ŻYDOW-
SKIEJ PADŁA OFIARĄ HITLEROW-
SKIEGO TERRORU.

STOWARZYSZENIE BYŁYCH
MIESZKAŃCÓW KRASNOSIELCA
W IZRAELU I U.S.A. 1996

The four tablets set on the wall of the synagogue at Krasnosielc in Hebrew, Polish, English and Yiddish

At the memorial site in Krasnosielc

Receiving a map of the area from the mayor of Krasnosielc, Miroslav Galinka

A reception at the residence of the president of Israel for members of Machal 1948, held in January 2003.

Back row from left to right: Machalniks: Murray Greenfield (USA), Sol Jacobs (Canada), Lionel Drucker (SA), Unidentified , Eddy Kaplansky (Canada), Unidentified, David Shachar (France), Maurice Ostroff (SA)

Front row left to right: Zipporah Porath (Machalnik USA), President Moshe Katzav, Smoky Simon (SA), Chairman of World Machal, Al Schwimmer (Machalnik USA and Chairman of Board of Israel Aircraft Corporation)

Receiving the honorary title of Friend of the Hitadrut, in the presence of the chairman of the Histadrut. Mr. Amir Peretz, the mayor of Ramat Gan, Mr. Zvi Bar and the chairman of the Ramat Gan branch of the Histadrut, Mr. Avi Galili

Chaya and David Shachar

Chaya and David's three children: Noam, Zohar and Lior

The generations of the Shachar family, 2005.

CHAPTER FOUR

From Poland to Paris

In May 1945, Germany surrendered unconditionally, and after six years World War II ended. Only 350,000 Polish Jews survived the war. They made up 10 percent of all the Jews of prewar Poland. Only 150,000 Jews came back from the extermination camps, and about 200,000 more returned from Russia. During the months after the war the Jews had the opportunity of returning to Poland, but they usually could not go back to their homes as in most cases these had been destroyed or occupied by Poles. A government committee established for matters of repatriation was in charge of advising survivors to settle in various regions of Poland. In Krasnoscielc, my hometown, Polish people took over the houses already in 1939, immediately after we were expelled. Upon our return from Russia, my family was sent to settle in Boza Gora, located in Upper Schlesia, a previously German area that was annexed to Poland after the war. At that time the Polish government decided to transfer the Germans who lived in that area to West Germany and to settle the place with Jews and Poles who lived in former East Poland, which had been annexed to Ukraine and Byelorussia. When we arrived at Boza Gora, 50 percent of its residents were Polish, 40 percent were Jews who had come there after the war and about 10 percent were Germans who had not yet left for Germany.

In 1946, I arrived in Boza Gora with my mother, my sisters and my brothers – Bronia, Leah, Yitshak, Malka and Elimelech. Aharon was not with us, as he had moved on to Germany. I started to work in Boza Gora in one of the Polish internal security units engaged in repatriation. We had to enter the homes of the German families with weapons for self-defense (we never actually used them) and evacuate them to make room for the Poles and Jews who did not have anywhere to stay. Most of these German families were weak and submissive. They were mostly women, old people and children, as the men had been recruited to the army, or worse – captured or deceased. They themselves had suffered from the soldiers of the Red Army, who committed acts of robbery and rape to avenge the horrible acts committed during the German conquest. Here was destiny reversing itself. After the reality of a horrible war, the Germans begged us not to hurt them while repeatedly swearing that they were not personally involved in harming the Jews.

In postwar Poland, anti-Semitism was beginning to rise again – some people said that it had never stopped. Some people who used to be members of the *Armja Krajowa* (the underground right-wing Polish organization) and other traditional anti-Semitic organizations aroused hatred against the Jews and spread rumors that the Jews were helping the Soviet Army take control of Poland. Jewish passengers were more than once taken off trains and murdered in cold blood. Pogroms were committed against them just one year after the war had stopped, such as occurred in the town of Kielce in 1946.

The wave of anti-Semitism became stronger after Poland was liberated by the Red Army and the Polish People's Army. Many of the twenty-five thousand Jewish soldiers and officers in it were appointed to security positions, such as town majors, intelligence officers, members of the security services and the like. Later, I also guarded the gate of the Gordonia movement "kibbutz." Like most of the Jews from Poland who survived the war, we too did not intend to stay in Poland for any length of time because of the rapid spread of anti-Semitism. In the meantime, the Zionist movements in Poland began to reorganize and grow. Secular movements like Hashomer Hatzair, Gordonia and Haliberalim, together with religious movements like Hapoel Hamizrachi, Poalei Agudat Yisrael and others sent representatives from Israel to various towns in Poland and to refugee camps in Austria and Germany. These emissaries spread Zionist propaganda and advised the young people to immigrate to Israel, and at the same time competed with each other to attract the young people to their respective movements. The movements established so-called "kibbutzim" in various places, where groups of young Jewish people carried on lifestyles similar to the ones in the kibbutzim to prepare them for life in Israel. Nevertheless, the British who governed Palestine prohibited entry and granted only a small number of visas, causing many people to enter the country illegally.

My mother wanted my brothers and me to join one of the religious Zionist movements, but she had to accept my decision to join Gordonia. I chose this movement in particular because of the significance they attached to principles of self-fulfillment, a value that was close to my heart. After attending a meeting in the town of Rzyzbach with Pinchas Lavon, one of the movement's founders, and listening to his instructive lecture I decided to join the kibbutz of the Gordonia movement. My sister Leah and my brother Yitshak decided to come with me. Malka and Elimelech stayed with Mother.

At that time my sister Bronia met Rabbi Isaac Goralnik, of blessed memory, a graduate of a Lithuanian yeshiva who had been in the USSR during the war, and they married. It was the first wedding in the family after the war and we were very excited.

The three of us – Leah, Yitshak and I – left Boza Gora and moved to live in the Gordonia kibbutz in the neighboring town of Walbrzych. This kibbutz was like an urban commune. We were about fifty men and women, aged sixteen to forty-five. All of us lived in the same building, ate together and worked in various jobs. Many of us, myself among them, worked in the Ministry of Defense, the Ministry for Internal Affairs and the Polish repatriation offices. I continued to engage in settling the area with Jews and Poles. In addition, once in a while I sold ice cream in the city park from an ice-cream truck. Like all the others, I put all of my income into the common money box – though I could not share my unlimited ice cream consumption with my fellow kibbutzniks.

Various activities and lectures took place on the kibbutz. The instructors were specifically trained for it at the movement's national headquarters in Lodz. We heard lectures about the history of Zionism, about the establishment of settlements in the Galilee and about the history of Deganya and Tel Hai. The instructors also made sure that we had a cultural and spiritual life. They taught us how to read Bialik and A.D. Gordon in Hebrew. We learned how to sing in Hebrew and how to dance Israeli folk dances. At the same time we underwent military training, where I was able to contribute my share. As a result of the know-how and the experience I had acquired in the Polish army, I was able to train my friends in the use of weapons.

Many of the members of the kibbutz wished to live life to the fullest. The will to enjoy life was especially strong among the survivors of the concentration and extermination camps. Paradoxically these people usually projected emotional strength and were less dispirited than us, the survivors of Russia and Siberia. These characteristics probably helped them survive the camps. We used to go out on trips, throw parties, sing and participate in ballroom dances. I had many friends among the male and female members of the kibbutz and I enjoyed the open and liberated atmosphere. For me it was the complete opposite of the strict religious life I had lived just a short while ago in my mother's home. Yet these extreme swings from one frame of mind to another confused and disturbed me.

In the spring of 1946 we were informed that Rabbi I. Herzog, the chief rabbi of Palestine at the time, had obtained permission from the Polish authorities to evacuate one thousand Jewish children, mostly war orphans, from Poland. At the time we all believed that the destination of this "Herzog Transport" would be Palestine. The four of us – Yitshak, myself, Malka and Elimelech – were eligible and we joined the transport – which delivered us in France via a lengthy stopover in Prague.

In the beginning, we were assembled in a fancy hotel in Aix-les-Bains, France, called Beau Site. Later on, the young children, including Malka and Elimelech, were left in Beau Site while the older children, including Yitshak and I, were transferred to Villa Richmond, a beautiful castle called Maison du Diable (the House of the Devil) because of the strong winds that blew on it.

About one hundred boys between the ages of thirteen and twenty lived in Villa Richmond. We were divided into groups according to age, and I was assigned to a class together with my brother Yitshak. Our classes were organized according to the strict regimen of studies that was customary in the Lithuanian yeshivas. The studies were held in Yiddish. During most of the hours of the day we listened to sermons and lessons in Torah, Mishna and Gemara and took part in classes on character development. Although the transfer to a strict lifestyle angered me, I proved myself to be a good student.

During our stay in Villa Richmond we had comfortable living conditions and enjoyed the sight of the beautiful castle. Each group of boys lived in a separate room. The food tasted good most of the time, although it was served in small portions – probably because of the ideological tendency of the Lithuanian yeshivas toward asceticism. Once in a while we left for trips in the vicinity and to ski in the Alps. The region amazed us with its beauty and we enjoyed the vacation town which was abundant with parks, wide meadows, lakes, fountains and statues. The town's wonderful scenery served as a romantic background for loving couples. A large and magnificent lake, Lac du Berger, a mountain with a snowy peak called Mont Revard and a river and mineral springs were all located close to the castle. The teachers of the yeshiva forbade us to meet the local girls, but could hardly enforce such a prohibition. Some of the yeshiva students who were caught spending time with the local girls were expelled from the school. As I was a naturally obedient youth, I did not engage in these activities.

A number of rabbis taught at the yeshiva, among them Rabbi Pogremansky who was respected as a Torah authority. During the war he served as a rabbi in a Lithuanian yeshiva and was known to have great influence on members of his community. Rumor had it that in order to cheer up the Jewish people of his town before they were shipped to the extermination camps, the members of the Judenrat would summon him to speak to the people. Before the Jews left on their last journey he would tell them the following parable:

"Once upon a time there was a man who had a glass-fronted display cabinet with a very expensive crystal dish in it. One day his maid turned the cabinet over by mistake and the crystal dish that was in it noisily shattered on the floor. The man was very upset. A little while later, in a large factory for crystal dishes, an employee accidentally overturned a cabinet containing many expensive crystal dishes, which shattered into many pieces. The factory employees were terrified they would be fired, but the owner calmed them down: 'Do not worry, the dishes that were in the cabinet were indeed made of pure and expensive crystal that cannot be obtained nowadays, but I am glad that they broke, as now I can collect all the pieces and fuse them with other crystal dishes in the factory, which will make them newer and shinier.' So too with the nation of Israel. Parts of the nation have died in previous generations, each man alone, but our generation is destined to cling together in order to sanctify the Holy One, blessed be He. He will fuse you in the future and make you into a new, improved generation." The parable that the Rabbi told the townsmen was one of those stories that brought comfort to the religious Jews during those difficult days and helped them in their belief that events depended on Divine Providence.

Due to his poor health, Rabbi Pogremansky was sent to the vacation town of Nice on the French Riviera for a short vacation. The purpose of the trip was for him to relax and ponder the words of the Torah. As destiny willed, I, of all the students, was chosen to accompany him. I assumed that it was due to my "skills" in public relations with the outside world, both with Jews and non-Jews. My job was to perform small services for him and take care of his visitors, especially members of the American Rescue Committee.

For about one month I lived with the rabbi in a fancy hotel on the promenade of a beach in Nice. Most of the time the rabbi sought solitude in his room and my job was limited only to running errands and to light services. Among other services, I brought him fruit and accompanied him on short carriage rides. Occasionally he shared with me his thoughts in Yiddish, afterwards asking me, "*Was zugt ihr* (What do you say)?" Since I usually did not at all understand what he meant I would nod politely and mumble something like, "These are indeed high-minded words." The rabbi was usually satisfied by this response. Rabbi Pogremansky lived an ascetic life – he ate his small meals in his room while I ate in a kosher restaurant near the hotel. A number of American Jews who came to Nice to gamble in the casinos ate kosher food in the same restaurant. They told me stories of casino gambling life. One was about a gambler who committed suicide after losing a large sum of money. These American Jews wanted to "educate" me and pointed to the Bible, which also contained stories about lust, corruption and exploitation. I was embarrassed facing the contradictions surrounding me – on the one hand, the rabbi's holy words and, on the other, the doubtful stories told by the guests from America.

My time spent in Nice was as water to a wilting flower. The pubs, the gambling clubs, the peaceful blue sea, the warm sun and the loose atmosphere met me upon my arrival in the vacation town of Nice and shook my hungry soul, aching as it was for the wonders of the world.

One day the Peace Festival was held in Nice, a spectacular and colorful event during which bundles of flowers were fired from the ships' decks and young women with short skirts paraded on the beach. The entire town, residents and tourists alike, celebrated the event. During this time I also became acquainted with the chief rabbi of Nice, who was considered relatively liberal. He contacted me and invited me a few times to his home, probably because I was accompanying Rabbi Pogremansky.

One day I met a Hebrew-speaking young man who told me that he came from Israel, where he had taken part in the Etzel Organization's bombing of the King David Hotel in Jerusalem. Etzel is a Hebrew acronym for "National Military Organization" – an underground military organization established in Jerusalem on April 10, 1931, by commanders who left the Haganah. His story greatly impressed me. It did not take long for us to become close friends and we spent many hours together. But one day when I returned to my room I discovered that all the money I received from the Rescue Committee to buy fruits and vegetables for the rabbi was gone. The hotel doorman told me that the "friend" had asked him for the key to my room, and since the doorman had seen us together many times, he agreed to the young man's request and gave him the key. I was very hurt by the betrayal and felt the pain of losing the money. I was too ashamed to tell anyone about it other than the local rabbi, who out of the kindness of his heart gave me some money to cover my expenses. Two years later, while walking around Tel-Aviv, I suddenly encountered this "friend." I asked him whether he remembered the days we had spent together in Nice and was not surprised when he immediately ran away from me.

After a month's time Rabbi Pogremansky and I returned to the yeshiva. Throughout the time I spent in the yeshiva my brothers and I corresponded with my mother on a regular basis. In the beginning of 1947, my mother and my sister Leah were transferred to a refugee camp in the city of Bamberg, Germany. There they joined my brother Aharon, who was already in Germany. My sister Bronia and her husband moved to the Orthodox yeshiva in Bailly, near Versailles, France.

During that period, my oldest brother Yosef came to visit Germany. He arrived wearing an UNRRA (United Nations Relief and Rehabilitation Agency) uniform, and was a representative of the Israeli political party Poalei Agudat Yisrael. At the end of his tour in Germany he also came to visit our yeshiva, and brought gifts of chocolate and cigarettes with him. We had not seen one another for many years, as I had been only five years old when he had left Poland, so I was very excited to meet him. He stayed at Aix-les-Bains for a number of days. We spent a lot of time together and had many conversations. In one of our conversations I told him that I hoped to use the ideological training I received and the experience I acquired in use of weapons. His reply greatly surprised me. He told me that Israel had many people with military skills and it actually lacked those who had a trade. Yosef even tried to convince the management of the yeshiva to provide us with some vocational training, but unfortunately they did not show any interest in his proposal.

As time went by, Yitshak and I became increasingly frustrated about staying in the yeshiva, both because of its strict lifestyle and also because our request to learn Hebrew or French before our immigration to Israel was not approved. I believe that the opposition of the yeshiva managers came from their desire to eventually transfer us to the United States and not to Israel. The yeshiva offices had at this time received a number of applications from American Jewish couples to adopt war orphans.

In the spring of 1947, Yitshak decided to leave the yeshiva. He traveled alone to Paris without a passport or any identifying document. Upon his arrival there, he found lodgings in a cheap hotel and got a job manufacturing women's purses. He sent me a number of letters persistently pleading with me to join him, but I postponed my decision. I was afraid to travel alone while my pockets were empty, without a job or knowledge of the country's language.

Finally, in May 1947, I decided to go to Paris. When I arrived there, I joined my brother at the Volta Hotel, located in a poor, working-class neighborhood near the Place de la Republique in the center of Paris. We lived in a small room, without a bathroom, a kitchen or even a sink. We had to wash ourselves in a basin and for meals we ate eggs fried on the primus stove in the room. A short time after I arrived, I went to the Jewish Committee in town and received my refugee certificate and financial support from the American Jewish Joint Distribution Committee. Later on, my brother Yosef arranged another source of income for me. I registered at a religious kibbutz near Versailles as an external member and received a weekly food supply which included tins of sardines, chocolate, soup powder and few other items, as well as three hundred francs for pocket money. All I had to do in return was to come to the kibbutz every Friday, spend the weekend there and take part in the prayers during the Sabbath. It was difficult for me to give up on my days of freedom and return to a religious lifestyle, which suddenly seemed strange and distant to me, but the financial support helped me significantly during the first months of my stay in Paris. During that summer Malka and Elimelech also arrived in Paris. Elimelech was placed with Bronia, while Malka stayed with her girlfriends in Versailles.

A short while after my arrival, I decided to acquire a trade. I went to the Ministry of Labor in order to pass the psychotechnical compatibility examinations. I was surprised to discover that I passed the examinations. The clerks recommended that I choose one of the technological subjects to study. From the list of courses offered to me I chose to study in the first radio-electronics course opened after the war, even though I had no previous knowledge of the subject. In addition, I registered for an evening course in French and a preparatory course in the field of electronics.

During the free months I had before starting to study, I used to walk the streets of Paris. I wanted to familiarize myself with its sites and streets. The bridges and alleyways seemed magical to me. I attended exhibitions, concerts and movies with my brother. The movies I saw in Paris did not resemble at all the propaganda movies I had seen a few years earlier in Russia, and they gave me the opportunity to understand the exaggeration and falsification of the anti-capitalist Soviet ideology. In the evenings we often went out to cafés in the bohemian parts of the city. We especially loved listening to the chansonniers in the Latin Quarter and strolling through Montparnasse and Montmartre. Occasionally we went out to dance with young Jewish girls in Jewish Zionist clubs. Other times we took the girls to a movie theater or to an amusement park, and it seemed to me in those days that all Paris was dancing and having fun. Once again I was exposed to a new world which opened up horizons of limitless possibility. On the weekdays I studied, had fun and enjoyed myself and on the weekends I prayed for hours and practiced religion. It was very difficult for me to decide where I stood in the midst of all these contradictions. The most basic questions stumped me. I had to think over what to eat, how to dress and what to do with my spare time and I continuously sought the answer to the question, "Who am I?"

I decided to study radio electronics at ORT. In order to do so I had to first complete various prerequisite courses in math and science as well a course in French, as it was the school's principal language of instruction. I therefore registered for courses in these subjects, and dedicated all my time and resources to studying.

Studying with me were Polish, French and Moroccan men – mostly soldiers who had been discharged from the army. I was supported by a small scholarship from the French Ministry of Labor, which obligated me to work for two to three years wherever they would send me after completing my studies.

The time I spent in ORT was the most difficult period of my life up to that point, because of the intellectual effort I had to invest, the personal challenges that confronted me and the difficult financial situation. Despite the hardships, I was determined to succeed in order to eventually be able to come to Israel as a professional. This aim was always before me and inspired me to overcome all obstacles. After a few months of tremendous effort, perpetual stress and sleepless nights, I succeeded in conquering the material and my achievements started to show.

Yitshak and I lived in a small room without ventilation or electricity. The close quarters created a lot of tension, leading to recurring arguments. The small table in the room was not large enough for me to make the drawings that my studies demanded. One day an inkstand turned over and stained a drawing which I had been working on for a number of days and of which I was very proud. The incident was exaggerated out of proportion and I decided to leave and look for a room of my own. It was very difficult for me to take the step. In addition to the material dependence on my brother, he was the only person I was close to during my stay in Paris, but the need for a place of my own was the deciding factor.

I rented the cheapest room I could find: an attic on the eighth floor of a hotel. Every day I had to climb up and down the eight flights leading up to my room. Like my former room, my new one was also narrow. I did not have enough space to prepare my drawings, and sometimes I had to go to my friends' houses to do my homework. Nevertheless, at last I had my own private place.

The hotel was located in a lively part of town. Next to it was the Les Halles market and every day during the early morning hours the market sprang to life. Truck drivers drove in with trucks loaded with fresh meat and vegetables from the neighboring villages, which they unloaded with loud cries. Afterwards the merchants came and the drivers hurried to drink a shot of aperitif or some steaming frog-leg soup. Painters, accordion players, policemen and thieves came there too, resulting in a colorful orchestra of sights, smells and sounds.

I used to observe the events that took place in the market from the window of my room. Sometimes I went down to buy a baguette, some chopped goose liver, vegetables and fresh eggs and prepared a delicious breakfast for myself. Usually it was the only regular meal I had during the day. It was impossible for me to feel lonely facing that lively tumult; it kept me company during the long hours I spent alone in my little room. After breakfast I walked to school and began a full day of studies. I satiated my hunger with baguette sandwiches spread with goose liver which I had prepared in my room. In the evenings I returned to my attic and spent many hours in preparing homework. A Polish fellow named Wladek who had been released from the Anders Army and joined his parents who lived in France, helped me with my studies in French. In return I gave him some packages of chocolate which I had received from my kibbutz. My studies demanded all my emotional and material efforts.

My lack of knowledge in basic subjects, such as differential calculus, physics and electricity and the difficulty I had in learning the French language made me think about the limitations imposed on us in the yeshiva, especially the one forbidding the study of French. These prohibitions were imposed to prevent any influence from the outside secular surroundings, and they indeed made my adjustment much harder. In order to make up for all the things I did not know I had to gnash my teeth and put in extra work during the nights and weekends.

One day I was called to the blackboard in order to answer a question about electricity and trigonometry. I felt very embarrassed standing in front of the class. In my clumsy French I asked the honorable professor, "What do you mean…?" How amazed I was when the professor answered me with a verse from the Bible: "And the Lord opened the mouth of the donkey..." "Don't despair," he added in French, "soon you will start talking and understanding the material."

When I inquired later I discovered that the teacher, Professor Shapira, was a Jew who had arrived in France during the Soviet revolution. During his youth he studied in a Jewish school, and in France he completed his academic studies in technology.

Over the years Professor Shapira's prediction came true. In time I did learn the language and understood the material. In the end I completed my studies with satisfying grades.

Occasionally I encountered in the streets of Paris the *Clochars* (vagabonds), who were eccentric students or just weird bohemians. The *Clochars* chose to live without any possessions or a roof over their heads for ideological reasons. For five francs they were happy to lecture to people passing by on different literary or philosophical subjects. Many were against materialism and in favor of "returning to nature," as professed by Jean-Jacques Rousseau. I loved listening to these lectures. Back then – and to the present day – I was very fond of anti-materialist philosophies. I was glad to meet people who as a philosophy of life chose to be satisfied with little. Their ideas encouraged me and softened the feelings I had after the tribulations that I and my family and many others went through during the war.

On January 5, 1948, my mother, my brother Aharon and his wife Esther, of blessed memory, immigrated to Israel on the ship *Transylvania*. Aharon had married Esther a short while before. When they arrived in Israel, the three lived in a small apartment in Haifa and shortly encountered financial hardships. After a short time, Aharon and his wife moved to Kiryat Ata and my mother went to live in Haifa with Yosef, his wife Bracha and their two children. During this time my sister Leah married Haim Korman, a Holocaust survivor from Poland, and they immigrated to Canada. Malka and Elimelech moved to Israel as well.

In May 1948 the War of Independence broke out in Israel. Again I faced a conflict. On the one hand, I was in the midst of studies for which I worked very hard. I had been accepted to the school and was determined to succeed. On the other hand, it was clear to me that if I did not take part in the fight to save my country I would never forgive myself. After a lot of consideration I decided that I wanted to take part in the war. In my heart I disliked those Jews who came from Israel to France to study medicine and engineering and justified their staying in France by saying that they wanted "to prepare the foundation of doctors and engineers for postwar Israel." It seemed to me that they were wrong and that they misled others intending "to be killed in the tent of the Sorbonne" while their country was struggling for its existence. It should be said that my patriotic feelings were mostly a product of the education I received during my period of serving in the Russian-Polish army.

The first phase of studies at the school ended in the autumn of 1948. Students who chose to graduate at this point received a diploma, and according to the agreement were sent to work two or three years in places selected by the government or else they were required to pay for the scholarship they received during their studies. I decided not to publicize my intention to immigrate to Israel, but when the time approached I told my secret to Professor Shapira, as he was known as a Zionist. A few months later during my military service at Bir Asluj I was very surprised to receive the graduation diploma of the first phase of the course.

Once I decided to immigrate to Israel and take part in the War of Independence, I also tried to convince my friends to join me. We held passionate arguments on the subject, in which my friends raised a number of strong objections. It had not been long ago since we survived World War II, and it did not seem humane to them to risk their lives again. Another excuse raised by them was based on rumors of the degrading attitude of the *tzabarim* (native Israelis) toward the volunteers, according to which they viewed Holocaust survivors as nothing more than "human dust" or "cannon fodder" for the war against the Arabs. Apart from this, they did not deny that they were happy in Paris and satisfied with their lives, which only recently had started to show signs of stability and success. I maintained my unequivocal views that if we did not take part in Israel's fight for independence we would not be able to look ourselves in the mirror in later years.

My family was also against my decision. They thought that whoever traveled to Israel was risking his life. In addition, they believed that immigrating to Israel and joining the Zionist army diverted people from religion. A few days before the date set for my departure I went to say goodbye to my sister Bronia and her husband in Bailly. Rabbi Pogremansky, who also lived there, invited me to his lodgings to say goodbye. I was very touched by this gesture of this old and honorable rabbi. With pleasure I joined him in his walk around the beautiful gardens near the castle. While we walked slowly in the gardens, he suddenly started to dissuade me from my plans. Speaking of God, the heavens and divine powers, he tried to convince me that joining the Zionist army contradicts God's will and Jewish family values and history. That night I could not sleep. However, I got up the next morning with the firm decision to continue with my plans. I believed that if I regretted my decision, I would never be able to maintain my self-esteem again. I can't deny, however, that the words of the rabbi made a lasting impression on me.

Though alone in my struggle, my resolve remained firm, until eventually I affected Yitshak with my decisiveness. In May 1948, we both went to sign a volunteer agreement for a period of a year with the Israeli Army within the framework of Machal, a Hebrew abbreviation for "Volunteers from Abroad."

At the end of the month I went with Yitshak to a training camp of the Haganah in the Grand Arenas Camp in Marseille. Jews from many countries came to this camp, and for two weeks we all went through exhausting combat training. We practiced using weapons and simulating combat in thorny mountainous areas similar to the Israeli terrain. The commands were given to us in Hebrew and translated into Yiddish, French and other languages. The Hebrew I had learned in my parents' home helped me to understand the commands. The instructors, members of the Palmach, seemed to me to be a successful model of the future Jewish nation, a model of glorious warriors. Even when it was most difficult, I never complained and cheered myself up with the thought that I was on a holy mission for the State of Israel.

CHAPTER FIVE

In the Palmach

The training camp at Grand Arenas ended in the month of June 1948, and Yitshak and I returned to Paris. From there we planned to go directly to Israel, but international events required that we proceed with caution. The war's first truce had just been declared, and UN inspecting delegations were positioned in ports and airports to prevent immigrants of military age from entering Israel. Therefore the members of the Haganah succeeded in deceiving the UN inspectors in various ways. They prepared a fake passport for me, according to which I was a journalist for *La Figaro*.

We landed at the Aerodrome Airport in Haifa. We were lucky that during passport control the inspectors did not notice our fake documents. We exhaled with relief and for the first time breathed the Israeli air. I was finally standing on the soil of my homeland. It is difficult to describe the exhiliration and the exaltation of spirit I felt. A very old and cherished dream had finally come true. Yet my joy and excitement were mixed with the fear of the unknown: fear for my fate as I entered into battle, and fear for the State of Israel, whose precarious future hung in the balance.

From the airport we were taken in buses to the old Technion building in Hadar Hacarmel. The next day I asked the representative of the Haganah who was in charge of our absorption for permission to visit my mother who lived in Haifa. Almost two years had passed since I had last seen here, and I was disappointed to find out that he rejected my request. "From now on you are recruited," he informed me coldheartedly. "There is no time for family sentiments." This reply was probably a result of the policy of the military authorities, but it also reflected the insensitive attitude of the residents of Israel toward Holocaust survivors, a patronizing and degrading attitude which I encountered more than once in my first years in Israel. In many cases the residents treated the survivors with pity mixed with disgust, as if they blamed us for not having the sense to immigrate to Israel in time, for marching to our deaths as "sheep led to slaughter," or even worse – for surviving the Holocaust only because we were egoistic manipulators or collaborators. This attitude embittered and frustrated many immigrants as they sought to build a new life in Israel.

The next day we were taken to a training camp in Kfar Yonah. Since, when still in France, I had declared that I was trained in the field of electronics, they first sent me to the communications corps and my brother Yitshak was sent to infantry. I immediately appealed because I wanted to serve in a combat unit, and under no circumstances would I agree to be separated from my brother Yitshak. The member of the selection committee who represented the communications corps tried to insist on my assignment but I remained firm, and eventually I was sent to serve in a combat unit with Yitshak.

The unit we joined had about one hundred people, most of whom were Polish and Romanian, and our commanders were native Israelis, mostly members of kibbutzim. We had to serve as a replacement force for soldiers of the Eighth Battalion of the Negev Division of the Palmach. This division defended the outposts in the Negev, and its forces were depleted while the battles were taking place.

At Kfar Yonah we went through exhausting combat-training exercises from dawn to dusk. The training exercises taught us how to fight and use the weapons and ammunition of the IDF – Sten guns, Bren guns (automatic machine guns), MAGs (German automatic machine guns) and grenades. After training sessions we listened to lectures about Zionism. Because I knew Hebrew better than my friends it was easier for me, and I often translated our commanders' orders for them. Unfortunately no attention was paid to helping the different cultural groups coalesce, and as a result alienation prevailed among us for many months.

After two months of training, in the beginning of August 1948, we climbed on trucks and rode to the Negev region, which at that time was under Egyptian siege. Despite the variety of terrains I had managed to see during the eighteen years of my life, here new landscapes were revealed to me. Yellow was the salient color, and it seemed that the sand and dust were infinite. When we arrived at Be'er Tuvia, a moshav that the Haganah used as a base for the southern troops, two guides joined us, and late at night they ordered us to arrange ourselves in a column so that we could cross the Egyptian front lines. They warned us about the Egyptian soldiers posted in the region and ordered us to preserve absolute silence. They explained that even the smallest noise could expose us and result in our capture. Before we went on our way one of the guides, who was a scout in the Palmach and wore an Australian hat, spoke to us. He talked about the daily "combat sheet" of the Givati Division, among the members of which were Aba Kubner and Beni Marshak. The title "Death to the Conqueror" was displayed on the sheet in large, bold letters. The scout elaborated:

"Free yourselves from this slogan. It was copied from the battlefields of Europe and related especially to two totalitarian regimes – the Nazi and the Soviet – which could not exist side by side on earth and therefore it was clear that peace could exist only if one of them was annihilated. On the other hand, here in Israel we are in the midst of a conflict with another nation, and eventually we will have to live together, side by side." And he immediately added, "Loving your homeland does not mean hating your enemy." Until today I remember the way his words pierced my spine in a shiver. They undermined my well-inculcated conceptions, but I remained thankful for his ideas, which helped me form my political-moral outlook on life. I hold these same beliefs to the present day.

The time had come for us to begin the operation. We held the weapons in our hands but the lack of organization was obvious in every step we made. We went on our way full of fear of the unknown. Every once in a while single shots were heard followed by an order to fall flat on our faces, but nothing else happened. We progressed without encountering any Egyptian soldiers, and in the early hours of the morning we arrived safely at Kibbutz Ruhama, where the headquarters of the Palmach divisions was located and which served as a center for the Israeli forces in the besieged Negev.

The soldiers of the Negev Division who had been placed together with the young settlers at Ruhama and other settlements had succeeded in preventing the Egyptian conquest of the settlements and had fortified them as commanding positions. We had to assist in defending these points and act against the invader. In addition, we were required to defend the water lines at these points and to prevent sabotage by the Bedouins. The Bedouins would occasionally blow up the pipes, both as acts of hostility and because they wanted the water for themselves and their herds.

When we arrived at Ruhama, I met a few fellows who I knew from France. On French soil we had served together in the French Commando Unit, which was established by an non-Jewish officer named Difre (Teddy Eitan). Eitan served in the Foreign Legion in French Africa and eventually came to Israel. At a certain point he convinced the commanders of the Haganah and the Palmach to let him establish a unit of French-speaking soldiers. With their approval he established a unit in France of about one hundred men, among whom were Jews from North Africa and Poland, as well as a significant number of Jews who had fought in the Spanish International Brigade and then stayed in France after the Republicans' defeat. There were also a number of people who were not Jewish. Because I had served in the French Commando Unit while in France, I was offered to rejoin the unit in Israel.

For a while I trained in the French Commando, but I very quickly discovered that I did not like its members. They liked to talk about sex and were proud of their conquests, had they really happened. There were incidents of drunkenness and violence. When I had the opportunity to switch units at the end of the training period I asked to return to the Eighth Battalion under the command of the native Israelis.

From Ruhama we moved to Kibbutz Gvulot, which was established in 1943 and most of its members were young people who had emigrated from Turkey. In the kibbutz we went again through a series of grueling training exercises, which included exhausting runs through the sands under the hot desert sun. A lot of tension existed between us and the members of the kibbutz. They refused to share the water and food with us. In order to avoid unnecessary arguments we ate only the food supplied to us by the Palmach in two separate shifts in the kibbutz dining hall. Even the female members of the kibbutz whom we tried to contact treated us arrogantly and suspiciously. The members of the kibbutz, both boys and girls, who were brought up in Achdut Haavoda (a socialist Zionist party originally founded in 1919 by Ben-Gurion) and were members of the Palmach youth groups separated themselves socially and politically from others who were outside their small circle. They treated those who were not brought up like them according to the values of Achdut Haavoda with reservation. We, who came to Israel as volunteers with a wish to contribute, were deeply hurt by this alienating and patronizing attitude and felt very frustrated.

The August sun was very hot and we continued with exhausting training exercises. One day during the training, the Palmach commander led us to a small piece of land where Bedouins grew white and green watermelons. After he talked to one of them and gave him a small piece of paper, he told us: "Guys, take a break and enjoy the watermelons." After running across the desert as heat waves hit us from all directions and the small quantity of water remaining in the canteen was almost boiling, those watermelons tasted like the fruit of paradise. When we had quenched our thirst, the commander revealed the contents of the note: "We will eat eight watermelons. Ben-Gurion will pay for them." We ridiculed the naiveté of the Bedouins who considered Ben-Gurion as omnipotent, but our commander became serious. "So you do not believe that Ben-Gurion can pay for the eight watermelons?" he asked.

On another occasion we stole a sheep from a local herd and built a campfire according to the famous campfire tradition of the Palmach. In addition to the pleasure of eating the delicious meat and the exhilaration of the adventure, the event was significant because of the new self-image we acquired. At last we were acting exactly like people who had always been in the Palmach.

After a month of training in the kibbutz, I and two other guys were chosen to be in the "mortar team." As I knew Hebrew well – relative to my friends – I was chosen to head the team.

The three of us were sent to a mortarman course at Kibbutz Nirim. A short while before our arrival the kibbutz had been attacked by Egyptians, and as a result most of its members were still living in bunkers. I will never forget my impressions of Kibbutz Nirim and its members. The kibbutz was a pile of ruins. Its members, as mentioned before, lived in bunkers and there were barbed-wire fences around the kibbutz. One day when I was wandering around, I noticed a young man in shorts, with a wild forelock of hair on his forehead, riding a brown horse around the outer fence. Over the years I found out that the young man was named Bren. He was later to become Major-General Eden, but back then he was the commander of the Kibbutz Nirim region. In spite of the harsh reality I encountered in Nirim, I could see their tremendous pride and confidence – hallmarks of the nascent Jewish state.

We were training with a heavy, three-inch mortar which was designed for firing long distances. Only a few mortars of this size were used in the Negev and they were transferred from one place to another, depending on the need. Our training included running under the hot sun carrying a mortar on our shoulders – one fellow carried the barrel, the other the base and the third accessories. As time went by, I became especially close to one of the two fellows who had come to Nirim with me. We called him "Herbert the *Yekke* (a Jew of German origin)." Although Herbert did not know any Hebrew, we were able to communicate a little in Yiddish and English. I admired him very much because he excelled in "manly" fields – judo, karate and riding motorcycles. Blue-eyed Herbert, who was trained as a paramedic, a brave guy with a lot of personal charm, was the only member in the unit who could conquer the heart of Judith, a native Israeli member of Kibbutz Gvulot.

The training at Nirim lasted ten days and after completing it we were sent to an additional training exercise at Kibbutz Tzeilim. After our training was over, we were sent to the final destination – a command high point that overlooked the road from Auja el Hafir to Beer Sheva. The command high point, which was not far from Kibbutz Revivim, was called Bir Asluj. It was erected on a treeless mountain top, overlooking the Negev's hilly regions. This area was very important strategically because of a valuable well and a small airport left by the British. A customs police building built by the British was there too. The British transferred the building to the Egyptians before their evacuation, but in June 1948, the police building was captured by the Eighth Battalion. The soldiers who arrived there did not know that the Egyptians had booby-trapped the building, resulting in the loss of many lives.

The position's commander, a member of the Palmach from Kiryat Haim, was called "Stinger" by everyone. A number of infantrymen, including my brother Yitshak, also manned the commanding high point, and still others defended it with Bren guns and MAGs. The team headed by me was put in charge of the mortar which operated as the only long-distance weapon (up to fifteen-hundred meters). We settled on the mountain top and viewed the hilly region beneath us. We had to be on shooting alert day and night. Egyptian convoys occasionally passed at the foot of the hill. We did not have aiming equipment, so we followed the orders of the commander and fired at will. Often we saw that the Egyptians stopped or went back because of the shootings, which indicated that we had hit them. When the Egyptian forces fired back, we stayed in the bunkers. We were lucky that the Egyptians were afraid to engage in actual combat, perhaps because they thought that the our force was larger than it really was or because they were afraid of the heavy mortar.

In order to protect ourselves we lived in trenches dug in the mountain. Herbert and I dug a foxhole – a small trench – where we lived in very close quarters. The third team member found a hiding place in the adjacent trench. The summer hit us with all its might. It was very hot in the Negev and we had almost no drinking water. The sand penetrated all the pores in our bodies and in no time we were covered with sores. We showered only when we could travel in a pickup truck to Kibbutz Revivim. At Revivim the members treated us again in a reserved way. Only Rochale, the kibbutz nurse, had a special corner in her heart for us. Rochale lost her husband during the bombardment of the booby-trapped police post at Bir Asluj. Of all the members of Kibbutz Revivim, I can only remember her favorably for her sympathy toward us.

In the bunker which served as a dining room, we ate bread, cans of sardines, vegetables and cheese. Only on rare occasions when it seemed that quiet prevailed did we dare to go up to the tent located on the mountain slope and dine in the fresh air. Our uncontrolled overeating sometimes caused stomach aches and headaches. The heat and the dirt, as well as the angry arguments that would break out between us, did not improve our well-being. Occasionally the howls of the jackals bumping into the empty tins we had left behind broke the desert silence. The sounds emanating from the darkness magnified our worries and fears.

In our new position we were forced to cope with incessant boredom. We would lie down for days without any amusement to distract us. To lessen the boredom, some of my friends played cards but I did not join them. Only the old gramophone playing scratched records provided some entertainment during our days and nights. I listened to the songs of Yaffa Yarkoni and Shoshana Damari again and again until I learned to like and appreciate them. The unit also had a radio, but since it was used only for wireless communication it was kept in the commander's bunker and we could not use it.

Under these circumstances, overloaded with spare time, Herbert told me his unique and fascinating life story. He was born in the city of Koln in Germany to liberal parents. The lifestyle, the upbringing and the atmosphere in his parents' home were similar to the ones in his neighborhood. When the Nazis came to power, they arrested his father, who Herbert had not seen since. In order to remove any political suspicion from her son, his mother registered him at a school for nationalist youth which was part of the Nazi Party's youth movement. When he reached the age of sixteen, Herbert joined the German army and went into combat. In one of the counter attacks against the American army in Ardennes, Belgium, he deserted. After the war, he was reunited with his mother. The representative of Etzel (the National Military Organization) in Europe tried to convince him to immigrate to Israel. When Herbert discovered his origin, he decided to adopt his original identity, became an enthusiastic Zionist and immigrated to Israel alone. Once in a while, he went to visit his mother who remained in Germany.

Herbert loved the military atmosphere very much and was always looking for adventure. One day we saw an Egyptian position with a flag flying on it. I translated for Herbert when he asked the commander for a gun with a silencer so that he could kill the position's sentries, confiscate their flag and cause harm to enemy morale. He was really disappointed when his offer was rejected. A short while later I was called to the position commander. "Listen, David," he said to me, "we do not know who your trenchmate is. There is a great possibility that he was planted in the unit by the Germans or the Arabs. We suspect that his excessive enthusiasm and his strange ideas are intended to cover it. As someone who spends a lot of time with him, you must know that he can hurt you, so be careful!" I can't deny that the commander's words gave me cause for worry, and from then on it was difficult for me to fall asleep next to Herbert. I did not stop liking him, but I asked myself again and again what his real identity was. It took quite some time until I accepted his purity of heart and good intentions again.

Many of the unit's soldiers were ex-partisans and Holocaust survivors who suffered from mental distress that they brought with them "from there." They complained a lot about the conditions and especially about the way the native Israelis treated us. Frequently they uttered the familiar words – "we were brought here to be used as cannon fodder." Though there was a certain amount of truth in their words, their interpersonal ways of thinking were indeed distorted in the Holocaust. One day I found out that one of the members of my unit had started to dig an underground tunnel, so that if the Egyptians conquered the commanding position, he would be able to escape through it to the desert. That was how he used to hide in Warsaw's sewer canals, a behavioral pattern that repeated itself in this command position in the Negev. He hid his intentions from most of the people with him and especially from our commander because he was afraid of being ridiculed.

Another time a number of members of my unit, who could not take the hostility and the contempt shown by our commander, decided to kill him. I went to the commander and warned him. He then called a meeting with them, after which they gave up the crazy idea. Yet after this event some men in the unit called me "informer" – a derogatory name for Jews who collaborated with the Germans or Russians and who would hand their friends over to the enemy for just a piece of bread. The men did not actually hurt me, but I felt humiliated. These kinds of events reflected the feelings of alienation that prevailed among the unit's members.

The soldiers who were with me on the mountain called the Palmach members "ruffians" because of their shorts and sandals. It was difficult for them to believe that these "ruffians" would eventually succeed in overcoming the organized and strong Egyptian forces. I, on the other hand, appreciated the native Israelis very much for their heroic struggle to establish the State of Israel. It was their practical approach that captured my heart. They fought when necessary and during the lulls they knew how to spend their free time. I also liked their humility. I was impressed by the simple clothes they wore, by the fact that they were satisfied with little food and by the lack of formality between soldiers and their commanders. I tried to explain to my comrades that the Holy One, blessed be He, was very benevolent toward us Jews, and that while most of the nation suffered hellish torments in Europe, its other part lived in Israel and acted for the country's resurrection, out of love for the nation and the homeland and in a spirit of total self-sacrifice.

One day we planned to carry out a patrol deep within Egyptian-held territory. The patrol was longer and more dangerous than usual and we hoped to expose the enemy's weak points. The commander decided that my brother Yitshak would join the patrol, but I worried a lot about his well-being. I went to the commander to express my worries, and asked to join the patrol with Yitshak. The commander accepted and eventually we, five armed men together with Yitshak, left for enemy territory. After a few hours we returned safely to our position. The incident made the commanders give some thought to whether brothers should be permitted to serve in the same combat unit.

One day I noticed soldiers riding in a pickup truck carrying differently sized pipes. Every day thereafter they drove back and forth. This evoked my curiosity and I made inquiries. It turned out that the soldiers in the pickup truck were trying to mislead the Egyptians into thinking that we had a large quantity of cannon.

One day a heavy vehicle carrying a water tank turned over and crushed the head of one of the soldiers. My friend Herbert, who had been a combat paramedic in the past, volunteered to escort the wounded soldier to the medical bunker in Kibbutz Revivim. The old doctor who received the wounded soldier passed out immediately when he saw him but Herbert stayed cool and acted very proficiently. The soldier died from his wounds a short time later but Herbert was very much appreciated for his action, and the army decided to assign him as the head paramedic in the Central Hospital in Ruhama, where most military medical operations took place. He left our unit and instead another soldier joined me in the trench. After the war Herbert remained in Israel. He married and raised a family, served in various units of the IDF and made it to the rank of major. Herbert and I have stayed in touch until today.

In November 1948 we had our first leave from the military. I went to see my mother, who lived in Haifa with Yosef and his family. Since July, when I had immigrated to Israel, until November I had only been able to communicate with my family through letters. I had learned what had happened to the rest of my family through my mother's letters. My brother Elimelech and sister Malka had also come to Israel. Elimelech joined the Ponovitch Yeshiva in Bnei Brak and Malka joined a religious settlement of the Aliyat Hanoar (Youth Immigration). My brother Yosef had returned to Israel from his mission in Europe.

Now in the War of Independence my mother had three sons serving in the army – Yitshak and I in the Negev Division of the Palmach, and Aharon in the Alexandroni Division.

My brother Aharon, who joined the Alexandroni Unit during the War of Independence, stayed with his unit in the southern part of Israel. One day he received a telegram informing him that his wife had given birth to twins, and his commander made an exception and authorized him to go and visit her. The next day, during his absence, his unit took part in the attack on the Iraq el Sudan police station (near Kibbutz Negba) and almost all his company members were killed in a bloody and cruel battle. His life was saved by miracle.

In one of my letters to my mother I wrote that I was aware of the fact that three of her children were in battlefront, and therefore it must be quite difficult for her – especially after she had lost her husband, two of her children and all her extended family in the Holocaust. I explained to her that I had decided to join the Israeli army because my conscience dictated it. My mother replied to me in her letter: "Dear David, first of all, from the bottom of my heart I hope that you and all your brothers will get through the war safely, and I pray for your well-being a number of times a day. Nevertheless, please do not find excuses for your decision to become a fighter, and you must do your job as you deem necessary. My children who were killed during the Holocaust died in vain, but if, God forbid, something happens to you too, it will be for a cause that you believe in, which is also the wish of the entire Jewish nation – the establishment of the State of Israel." This courageous letter demonstrated my mother's character. Although she was an Orthodox Jewish woman from a non-Zionist background, she respected the feelings and decisions of others, even those of her own children.

In November, as mentioned before, I finally went to see my mother. To the best of my memory, the meeting was very exciting. It became clear to me that my mother's economic situation was quite difficult and her emotional condition was pretty low, too. After she capably led the family throughout the long and difficult war years, she suddenly found herself depending on others. She could not communicate with her grandchildren, because they spoke only Hebrew, and the loneliness that befell her was a great burden.

During that period I also visited Frieda, my friend from the days I studied in the school in Zagorsk. Frieda lived in the Ajami neighborhood of Jaffa. I remember well from my visits to Tel Aviv back then how I was amazed to see the stark difference between the vigorous city life of entertainment and enjoyment and the atmosphere of war and harsh conditions prevailing only a few miles away. During my leave I was also one of the partygoers, and together with Frieda I went out to the coffee shops in Tel Aviv and had a great time. After I returned to my base at the command high point, I carried on a correspondence with Frieda and was happy to find a soulmate to miss during the long hours I spent on duty.

A short time after my vacation the battles in the Negev ended and after six weeks of negotiations, on February 24, 1949, a cease-fire was signed with the Egyptians. According to the agreement the Gaza Strip remained part of Egypt and the rest of the Negev became part of Israeli territory. It was also agreed that the ceasefire lines would be declared as the truce lines and the Nitzana region would remain demilitarized.

The command high point where I served lost its strategic importance and we were transferred elsewhere. At the time the Negev lacked people who were skilled in the radio and electronics field. Due to my background in the field, I was attached to the technical team of the Communications Corps in Beer Sheva, commanded by Lieutenant Colonel Egon Ron, the commander of the technical unit of the IDF in the Negev.

My brother Yitshak was transferred to an infantry unit in the Dahariya region near Hebron, and after many years of serving side by side our paths separated. Yitshak told me once that he missed the vigorous life he tasted in Paris, yet nevertheless I knew that he was proud of his part in the War of Independence and in his contribution to the establishment of the State of Israel, and he still likes to tell his children and grandchildren about those exciting days.

A short while after I joined the Communications Corps, Egon Ron registered me in a program to learn how to repair and operate the various communication devices in the area. The program took place at two technical bases of the Communications Corps near Tel Aviv, one in Sharona (today known as "Hakirya") and the other in Bnei Brak.

At that time I went to express my condolences to the mourners at the home of my mother's uncle, Dov Cohen, who immigrated to Israel during the 1920s and lived in the center of Tel Aviv. One of his sons, Refael, was killed in April 1948 during the battle over the Najada House in Haifa. Another son, Yosef, studied engineering in Belgium, and was later appointed to be the chief engineer of the Municipality of Haifa. My uncle, though religious, was very tolerant of his secular children and their decisions. I loved to visit there and enjoyed the Israeli and family atmosphere, which I missed so much. I also met my friend Frieda again, but when I found out that she was going to marry one of her neighbors we ceased contact.

The people who served in the Communications Corps, usually of German and British origin, I considered snobs. They dressed in suits and ties, went to concerts and dined in restaurants. Their culture and customs was absolutely different than those of the fighters I had fought with in the Negev.

One day during the study program, I collected a number of used spare parts from one of the warehouses that belonged to the Communications Corps. I took mostly those parts that had been damaged from being shaken by the rough rides on the road, such as outside spiral antennas. I intended to take them to my unit, which suffered a constant shortage of these spare parts, but I did it without asking for authorization. When I left the gate, the guard found the parts in my bag and after handing me over to the instructors, they decided to incarcerate me for the night. The next morning I was given a trial, where I presented all the bitterness that had accumulated in recent months to the Judging Officer Yeshayahu Lavie, who was also the base commander. Among other things, I protested against the difference between the easy service in Tel Aviv and that of the Negev. Not only were the poor soldiers endangering their lives, I said, but no one takes care of their comfort and needs. The base commander listened to my claims, acquitted me and even authorized new spare parts to be given to me so that I could take them to my unit.

When I returned to Beer Sheva, I was appointed supervisor of the laboratory. I was very proud, both because of the trust they showed in me and because I was being promoted less than one year since my arrival in Israel. I was very satisfied with my work. I knew that I was contributing to the army and to the state and I considered my duty as a mission. Combat units in the field would contact us when their equipment was not operating and we traveled there with jeeps to repair the damages. I remember my experience driving acroos the Negev in a jeep as a uniquely Israeli experience – this despite the fear of mines that the Bedouin placed in the dirt tracks. Sometimes acquaintances and family members came to visit me, especially my sister Malka. I loved taking them for patrols in the jeep so that they could also enjoy the prairies of the Negev and feel the wonderful sensation of postwar freedom.

In spite of the many victims claimed by the war, the victory over the Arab armies created an atmosphere of freedom and prosperity. Although austerity prevailed back in those days in Israel, the will to live overcame the difficulties and obstacles. An atmosphere of revival and creativity was felt throughout the young state. In Beer Sheva Hatzkel opened a branch of the famous Tel Aviv Kassit Café, which in Tel Aviv had become the meeting point for the literary group formed around the poet and publicist Natan Alterman. Habima (Israel's national Jewish theater) performed a new play by Yigal Mossinson, *In the Plains of the Negev*, which was based on the experiences of the playwright as an information officer at Kibbutz Negba during the War of Independence. The first volume of the Hebrew Encyclopedia was published at a festive ceremony which was held in the Habima hall. In those days the railway route from Tel Aviv to Jerusalem started to operate again after a long hiatus.

All the members of the Communications Corps' technical team, which included technicians, radio operators and code interpreters, were considered a technological and intellectual elite (a good control of the Hebrew language was required from the radio operators and code interpreters). My belonging to this elite group flattered me a lot and the rest of the group members considered me one of them. The "ugly duckling" syndrome that accompanied me when I first came to Israel took a positive turn – I had finally been accepted into the flock of the swans. We used to eat, sing, walk and party together.

The mistakes I made in Hebrew amused the group. For example, late at night, when I wanted to go to bed, I asked my friends to "make the night" – a direct translation from the Yiddish expression *machen nacht*, which implies, "may you sleep in peace." Since that time they used to call me "David Make the Night."

In early 1949 Egon Ron left the unit and I was appointed to replace him as commander of the technical unit of the entire Negev region. I was very proud of my new position, particularly because of my young age. I was only nineteen and had already been chosen for a senior technical position. (I knew, of course, about the shortage in senior professionals in this field). I worked hard to make the unit's operations more efficient. Among other things, I strengthened the antennas with telephone wires in order to improve the communication with the units in the fields.

In the meantime, the year of service I had signed up for within Machal had passed and I asked to be released from the army. Because of the pressure put on me by my commanders, I agreed to stay in my position a few more months, until my release in November 1949.

The army authorities let the fighters who took part in the conquest of Beer Sheva each choose one abandoned Arab house and take control of it. The unit commander suggested that I take over an old radio-equipment shop in Beer Sheva. Various strange pieces of equipment lay around the shop together with many cockroaches and insects. My friends in the unit offered their help in renovating the shop, but because of my plans to continue studying electronics and because of the negative personal connotations that accompanied the abandoned shop, I at length decided to refuse the offer.

As my release from the army approached I weighed the three possibilities I had been given when I signed the agreement with Machal in Paris. According to the first one, the Ministry of Defense would finance my traveling back to France to continue my studies; the second possibility was to stay in Israel and continue my studies toward a degree in electronic engineering; and the third, to be an ordinary new immigrant. I chose to stay and study in Israel with the financing of the Ministry of Defense as I was promised, but to my surprise and disappointment, the clerks of the Ministry of Defense refused to approve my application. They cited the policy of Levi Eshkol, the general manager of the Ministry of Defense: "The State of Israel is poor and it cannot fulfill the promises it gave you." "You are lucky to be young," I was told. "You survived the war healthy and in one piece. We wish you well and hope that you will be able to manage on your own." I was very disappointed that I could not study, and I was prevented from getting various jobs and promotions later on because I had not completed my academic and technical education.

In spite of the disappointment, I decided to stay in Israel. The decision came mainly because of the obligation I felt toward my mother and because I felt the need to help support her. She had rented a small apartment in a religious Haifa neighborhood on Arnon Street, not far from Yosef's apartment. She did not have any source of income back then, both because of her age and because in her community it was not considered modest for a woman to work outside the home. My sister Malka came to live with her again and Yitshak also joined them later. In deciding to remain in Israel, I was thereby expressing my identification with my homeland and my family.

CHAPTER SIX

Acclimatization in Israel

Having elected to remain in Israel upon my release from the army in 1949, I had to decide where to settle. I had the possibility of joining Kibbutz Kiryat Anavim, where most of the former members of Kibbutz Gordonia had settled. I opted instead to return to my mother in Haifa, whom I knew it was my responsibility to support. As I was in urgent need of an income, I accepted the first post offered me by the Employment Bureau immediately following my discharge, and so soon found myself taking part in the installation of water pipelines in the Negev. I was required to carry buckets full of sand and to work long hours under the scorching sun, but the pay I received was necessary to support my mother. During that period I was permitted, under special circumstances, to live in the camp in which I served. Later on I moved to the Soldiers' House in Beer Sheva.

For one month I installed pipelines, and then at the beginning of 1950 I obtained employment worthy of my skills and professional training, at a telephone repair workshop in downtown Haifa. The technical manager of the workshop had learned the vocation under the British postal services. He proved to be pedantic and fastidious in the most tedious of technical matters and working in his company required both tolerance and restraint. I was further burdened by the living conditions in my mother's home, a small, one-room apartment not more than fifty square feet, shared by the four of us – my mother, Malka, Yitshak and myself. It was with great difficulty that we squeezed four beds inside it. It hadn't been long since the whole apartment had served as the building's laundry room. Outside of it, in a small, unventilated corner, were located the shower and kitchenette and in order to use the bathroom we had to leave the apartment. Religious customs, which prohibited turning on the light and radio on Saturday, or eating anything not kosher, and to which I had to adhere to protect my mother's respectability, also weighed heavily on me. I had already become accustomed to an independent, secular way of life, and I was in the midst of developing my own personal direction. This reversion to the family hearth was very bothersome to me and it did not live up to the expectations I had developed for myself. In spite of all this, I endured.

During that time new immigrants, especially former soldiers, were offered the opportunity to purchase houses that had been abandoned by Arabs. We could have purchased a beautiful apartment in Abas Street on the Carmel mountainside, looking out to the sea, but my mother insisted that she wouldn't live in a house whose former tenants abandoned it or were driven out. I identified with my mother's position, although I couldn't help feeling some regret as many of my friends, former members of the Machal, received various benefits from the state while I remained in our small cramped apartment.

Sometime later the workshop in which I worked fell into financial difficulties and I was laid off. In those days there were great shortages and we all went through harsh times. We had to stand in line day after day to receive food rations. My brother Yitshak got accepted into an accounting course paid for by the Employment Bureau, and upon finishing, he began working as a bookkeeper in the Haifa port. I refused to give up the profession I had acquired in France, and so maintained my stubborn search for suitable work.

Grudgingly, I turned to Yeshayahu Lavie. He was a chief communications officer whom I had met back in the days when he served as commander of the radio and electronics lab in Sharona. I asked for his help, and he offered me a job in the Galei Zahal broadcasting station that had recently been constructed on the Carmel Mountain. I accepted his proposal gladly, and began working as a technician for Galei Zahal. Among other things I was in charge of examining the equipment during broadcast interferences.

Whenever there was a malfunction, I tried to repair it. Likewise I was responsible for maintenance on a daily, weekly and monthly basis. I worked in the company of Yona Peles, who studied electrical engineering at the Technion during that period. Years later, he became the first director of the Center for Educational Technology. Together we manned the post in shifts, twenty-four hours a day. For close to two years I worked at that station, except for one month each year, which I spent on reserve duty in the Communications Corps.

Close to my mother's place there was a repair shop for small electrical appliances. Bezalel, the owner of the shop, would occasionally pass malfunctional radios on to me. The small dining table became my work bench, and the blips and beeps emitted by the small radio instruments would fill the crowded apartment. I worked and saved every penny so I could pay my way to university. Regretfully, I was unable to sign up for regular studies in the Technion, so I opted to study electrical engineering through the British Council's correspondence school.

The difficult living conditions prevented me from investing much effort in the studies. The unbearably small family room stood in my way and curtailed my ability to commit myself to my studies. I hadn't given up on my ambition to begin normal studies at the Technion, and maybe even receive some financial support as others had. In the end, although I signed up for three years of study, I did not participate in the final exams, and I didn't receive the coveted degree.

In the social arena, in contrast to the academic, there was a gradual improvement in my situation. This came about to no small degree thanks to Bezalel, the owner of the repair shop, my neighbor and friend. Bezalel gathered a group of friends around him and became the living spirit of the group. Most of the fellows, former soldiers like me, asked nothing more than to enjoy life and get rid of the anxieties that had accumulated during their military service. Among the group's members were some girls, and every Friday we threw a party. A short while before the festivity we drove around in a truck and visited all of the girls' houses, taking them to the meeting place. The parties became the axis of our social life. We drank sodas and wine, we listened to records on the gramophone and danced tangos and waltzes. If we couldn't find a house to have the party in, we would go dancing in cafés.

One of the fellows, a young man named Abraham Hilman, was blessed with a particularly melodious voice. He delighted us with his singing, performing both classical and lyrical numbers. Abraham purchased a new gramophone and I built him an amplifier. With the improved machine we played classical music, especially arias sung by Enrico Caruso, Maria Callas and others. Abraham tried to accompany the performers on the records. In time, Abraham took singing lessons and became a respected cantor in Manchester, England. Because we didn't want to wear out the new gramophone, we still used the old one to listen to Israeli songs by Yafa Yarkoni and Freddy Dura, among others. Another fellow, Shlomo "Loksh (noodle)," won his nickname thanks to his great height, and the jokes he used to tell were given the descriptive name of "Loksh" jokes. My mother of course did not approve of me going out to parties on Friday nights, and upon my return she always asked me where I had been and what I had eaten, and expressed her hopes that I didn't come upon any nonkosher food. Because of the respect she enjoyed in the religious community I was careful not to argue with her about such matters.

When I was about twenty-one I decided I was old enough to consider having a serious relationship with a girl. From time to time I dated some of the girls from our group, and one day I arrived at one of the sabra's home on her birthday, dressed in a suit and tie and holding a bouquet. The door opened, and to my surprise, the "lady's" face twisted in contempt and she made it clear to me, under no uncertain terms, that she did not wish to go out with people whose behavior (a suit and flowers) indicated a certain "spinelessness" or "decadence." I was deeply hurt, but I learned my lesson, and for many years I did not approach a girl's doorstep holding a bouquet again.

I also met religious girls to whom I was introduced by my family. My family hoped that this would bring me closer to the traditional life.

Not far from our place, on Herzl Street in Hadar Hacarmel, there was a little café. I enjoyed sitting in the café and eating the Eastern European food that was served there – gefilte fish, jellied lamb's leg and other delicacies. From time to time I found partners for a game of chess.

The café was also frequently visited by Elka, a girl from Bezalel's group. One day, in the summer of 1951, she was accompanied by her girlfriend Chaya Shapira, a teacher in the Reali School. Chaya commanded my attention immediately.

Her face, clean of makeup, and her blue eyes, all radiated spirituality. I was glad to sit with the two girls and discuss literature and education. On our first meeting I was already impressed by Chaya's pleasant manner, her integrity, her intelligence and broad horizons. I felt that the interest was mutual and that we had "chemistry." In time I discovered that that meeting had been my first encounter with the woman who was destined to be my wife. Since our marriage Chaya and I have spent many happy years together, which have continued to this day.

Chaya was born to David and Esther Shapira on June 11, 1930, in the city of Pioterkov, near Lodz, Poland. Her mother Esther passed away during childbirth and a short time afterwards her father married a woman named Itka, who raised Chaya as her own. In 1938 her brother Menachem was born. The family was religious and their economic situation was quite humble. In 1935, the family immigrated to Israel and settled in Haifa. Chaya's father began work as a laborer with the Vulcan company. The family remained religious in Israel but Chaya refused to study at a religious school. As a result of her stubbornness her father received some biting remarks from his fellow party members, but despite this he respected her decision and Chaya applied to the Chugim secondary school. After graduation she joined the Haganah and served as a communications operator in the Carmeli Division. When she was discharged, she studied education in the Riali Seminary and in 1951 she served as teacher and educator at the Hadar branch of the Riali elementary school. She was quite successful in her teaching position. She lived with her family not far from us.

Chaya and I immediately found a common language. We quickly discovered that we both had a similar background. We were both born to religious, Polish families, and at some point in our lives we reached the conclusion that we did not wish to maintain the rigid religious lifestyle. Nonetheless, we were both careful not to demonstrate this publicly, as we did not want to hurt our families. We both exhibited a shared interest and knowledge of Judaism, history and literature. Apart from this we both served in the army in the War of Independence, Chaya in the north and I in the south. For the first time I felt that a connection had been forged between a young woman and myself which went far deeper than the common dating rituals.

We spent hours together. We frequented the cafés on Mount Carmel ordering soda, raspberry juice and falafel, as was the custom in those days.

We danced together in private parties at Gan Oranim, or at the Freddy Dura Club in Nahariya. From time to time we saw movies and plays – usually chosen by Chaya since she was an aficionado of these fields. I always trusted her good taste and I was glad to absorb some Israeli culture under her guidance. We also joined the Nature Lovers Society and enjoyed many hikes together in various places in the country. I took great pleasure in getting to know the hiking routes of Israel.

Chaya was also an excellent swimmer and on her initiative we used to go swimming at the beach in Bat Galim. From time to time I rented a surfboat and sailed it a couple miles off the beach. Even there, far from the beach, we found ourselves exposed to the searching eyes of the sailors serving at the navy base on shore. Their favorite pastime was to spy on sailing couples with a telescope.

My friendship with Chaya brought with it a bonus: her social circle. Most of her girlfriends were graduates of the teacher's seminary, and most of her male friends were engineers who had graduated the Technion. All in all, they made an impressive group of young, cultured working people, who had participated in the War of Independence and loved their country. They were interested in both Israeli culture and world culture. In the beginning I felt like a stranger in their midst, since they all had shared experiences from their time in the youth movements and the Palmach, and they had trained together and defended the country together. Also, the Hebrew I spoke was less polished than theirs. But I made it my aim to integrate myself into this group, which in many ways reminded me of my friends from my good days in Zagorsk and Rozan. In time, with Chaya's encouragement and help – for in addition to everything else she was a gifted teacher – I became well integrated into that society. I especially enjoyed the social get-togethers in the house of Yona and Shuki Kfiri. The company of Yona, who was also a teacher and educator in the Reali School, and Shuki, a Technion graduate and successful businessman, was very pleasing for me. We have maintained a strong connection to this very day with the Kfiri's and other friends in the Haifa circle.

Now, after many years, I can say with great satisfaction that my life with Chaya has brought me a blessed intimacy, three sons of which we are very proud, exceptional grandsons and granddaughters, and also a fast and efficient breakthrough in my integration and acclimatization to this country, her peoples and her vistas.

When our relationship was three years old we decided to get married. This was a period of great change for my family as well – in 1953 my brother Yitshak married a girl named Tova, a Holocaust survivor. Tova and her sister Judith were the only members of their family to survive the Holocaust. Over time Malka settled in the USA and Yitshak and Elimelech, in Canada.

Meanwhile, I quit my job as a technician at the Galei Zahal station, and in 1952 I began working as a civilian employee of Zahal at BMZA, an electronic equipment workshop in the navy base Kishon, located north of Haifa. This was a far more challenging occupation for me than my former job in Galei Zahal. In BMZA I dealt with running in new radars that had arrived from the American army which were considered to be the newest and most sophisticated equipment available. In order to succeed in my new position I read relevant technical material in my free time. My job instructor, Reuven Rotenberg, was head of the Army Radar Division. He and I became good friends. Reuven, a native of Egypt, was later appointed a lecturer in mathematics at the Technion. I appreciated and admired him greatly, and he remains in my memory as one of the most interesting people I knew. I formed good relationships with many of my other colleagues as well. As a person who used to be religious – and therefore an authority on Jewish tradition – I used to enthrall them with tales and aphorisms from the Bible and with Jewish lore. My friends, most of whom were devoutly nonreligious immigrants, were truly unfamiliar with the mainstays of Jewish tradition. Nevertheless, they enjoyed listening to me and hearing the messages of the Torah.

One day a technician of Austrian origin joined our unit. He was hired to work with us after presenting himself as an expert on radar. I soon discovered, to my dismay, that he didn't know a thing about radar. Furthermore, he aroused my suspicions with his bizarre behavior and his predilection for making notes. I approached the workshop commander with my suspicions, and military investigators arrived soon after. They put him under examination, and a short time afterwards the man disappeared from the unit and no one ever found out what happened to him.

After I was secure in my position at work, Chaya and I were able to fulfill our dream and get married. The date was set for April 7, 1954.

The marriage ceremony was held at the Carmelia Hotel in Haifa. It was a modest wedding, in the spirit of those days, and the food served was home-cooked by our own parents. The guests, no more than a hundred people, were a diverse crowd made up of family and friends – on my side, the guests were mostly new immigrants and religious, while Chaya's guests were mostly native Israelis and secular. Nevertheless, they all shared our happiness together. Our marriage illustrated for me the dichotomy that has accompanied me for many years – religion versus secularism, detachment and an alienated existence versus a home and sense of belonging. For me, union with Chaya symbolized my new path – one of belonging to Israel and to a free way of life where we made our own decisions. We enjoyed our guests and danced to the music of the hotel orchestra. We didn't engage a photographer for the wedding, but the next day we went to a studio for photographs.

After the wedding we went on our honeymoon. We stayed for a few days in the Eden Hotel in Tiberius, which was considered a fine hotel at the time. Immediately afterwards we went backpacking to the King Solomon Mines in the Negev. I had never spent the night sleeping in a sleeping bag under the desert sky and it was for me a cheerful and refreshing novelty. We both were dazzled by the desert scenery and the intense sensations it stirred within us.

After our honeymoon we returned to regular life and began to plan our future. We deliberated between moving to the kibbutz or staying in Haifa. We couldn't afford to buy an apartment in Haifa. However, to our great good fortune, Chaya's father won five thousand pounds in the lottery a short time before our wedding and he kindly helped us purchase an apartment. With his help and the lottery's, we bought a new apartment that was still being built in the Kiryat Eliezer housing complex. We remained for a short time in a rented apartment, and in the fall of 1954, when construction was complete, we moved into our new home.

We had some beautiful days. We didn't have a car, and in the apartment we had neither a phone nor even a refrigerator. But we were happy anyway. During the first months we used an ice box, and every morning, before going to work, Chaya had to stand in line to buy ice. Despite all this, I recall those months as a wonderful time of my life. We lived in our own apartment in an open and free way. Chaya continued to teach at the school, and I studied and worked. In 1958 I completed my matriculation certificate.

Our decision to remain in Haifa also meant that I stayed close to my mother. After all her children had departed, my mother was living alone once again. In those days a compensation agreement with Germany went into effect, and she began to receive a monthly stipend that provided her with minimal subsistence funds. Access to her house was blocked on Saturdays, so Chaya and I came to visit on weekdays. Once in a while she came to visit us.

In 1955 our eldest son, Zohar Haim, was born. The name Haim was chosen after my father Haim, may he rest in peace, and Zohar was chosen because we wanted a short, Hebrew name, with a bright, up-beat meaning. When he was about five weeks old, Zohar became sick with pneumonia. He was admitted to Rambam Hospital in Haifa. His life was in danger, and we feared for the worst. To our great relief, he recovered, and life again returned to normal.

In 1958 our second son was born. We called him Noam Moshe. Moshe – after my brother who died in a Gulag in Siberia, and Noam – because we loved that Israeli name. As often happens when an only child suddenly has a new contender for his parents' attention, Zohar was jealous of the newborn and suggested to Nehama, his devoted nanny, "Let's throw the baby in the garbage can."

I loved my children very much and I was very proud of them, but my work took up much of my time, and to my regret, I didn't dedicate enough time to them. I used to spend time with them mostly on the weekends. On Saturdays we went to the beach and walked along the green expanses that in those days covered the areas between the housing complexes in Kiryat Eliezer.

In the middle of 1954, after I had done well in my work with the navy, I was sent as a radar and sonar instructor to the naval training base at Bat Galim, not far from our modest apartment. I would arrive at work each day riding on a bicycle. At the training base I specialized in radars used on the British corvettes then in use by the navy. My pupils in the courses I taught were usually graduates of professional secondary schools, who were trained for the positions of radar, sonar and radio technicians. Once in a while I went out with my pupils to sail on navy ships in order to give them practical instruction on the equipment operating in the field. I was considered a very tough instructor, and at times I was nicknamed "The Inquisitor" by my students. Notwithstanding this, many of my pupils admitted to me that they really appreciated my teaching style. I would sometimes purposely create "malfunctions" in the electronic equipment so as to bring my students to a state of maximum readiness.

One of my good friends in the base, Captain Ephraim Talmon, joined the unit while he was studying electronic engineering in the Technion. Ephraim had already served in the navy before the founding of the state. I assisted him professionally and personally and apparently made a good impression. After he finished his studies, he was posted at Bat Galim as the commander of the electronics school's training base. I became Ephraim's assistant. He greatly appreciated me for my professional work, judging by the recommendation letters he later wrote for me. After I began working as a civilian in the navy base, I transferred there for my reserve duties as well, as an equipment engineer at BMZA. On one occasion while on reserve duty I set off on a month-long voyage on the ship K-22, on a mission of underwater mine removal. I functioned as the ship's maintenance engineer, but the commander decided to also employ us, the technicians, in routine jobs such as cleaning and even maneuvering the ship. I couldn't avoid the worrying thought of a possible malfunction, for I had no training in the steering of ships. Nevertheless, the voyage concluded without mishap, and life returned to normal with one more enriching experience under my belt.

CHAPTER SEVEN

From the City to the Border – Seven Years in Kiryat Shmona

A group of old friends from Kiryat Shmona have a custom of meeting about once a month for breakfast. Among the group's members are former Mayor David Morre, Director of Cultural Affairs in the City Council, Benny Ben-Eliezer, principal of the local school Ezra Danos, Raffi Malka, director of the Hula Textile Factory and Amnon Kroyzer, director of the local branch of Bank Hapoalim. Sometimes other friends from those days join us. At the end of each reunion I am again filled with gratitude for how well my fateful decision to move to Kiryat Shmona turned out. It was true that I was overly naïve and enthusiastic – for which I paid a price – but I have no regret over this chapter of my life in Kiryat Shmona.

The seed was already sewn in the year 1958. The Sinai Peninsula had been conquered in the Kadesh Barnea Operation (the Sinai Campaign), and Ben-Gurion, prime minister at the time, announced that the order of the day was the absorption of immigrants, distribution of the population to all parts of the country, and the support of frontier settlements. The majority of the residents in the development towns and the frontier settlements were new immigrants from North Africa and Middle Eastern countries, and it was crucial to strengthen them. The "Old Man" came out with a new catch phrase – "from the city to the frontier" – and set a public example by himself moving to Sdeh Boker in the Negev, far from the center of the country.

As members of the Mapai youth movement in the city of Haifa, Chaya and I set out in the year 1959 with a group from the movement to Sdeh Boker for a visit to Ben Gurion's "cabin." The meeting with him made a great impression on me. A tantalizing speech from the "Old Man" about the need to "Judaize" the Galilee and settle the Negev did its work on me. I felt that the right step for me to take at the time was to move to a frontier settlement.

Chaya and I faced a difficult decision. We both were climbing the professional ladder of our careers, and we enjoyed good pay and positions that suited our skills. I worked as an appreciated senior electronics instructor for the Ministry of Defense, and Chaya continued to teach as a senior educator in the Reali School. She loved her work and was very successful at it. To leave it all, to interrupt the development of our professional careers, to give up financial security, and to say goodbye to friends and family and take off on an adventure required great courage and daring. Many of our friends and family members thought our decision foolish and irresponsible and tried to dissuade us from taking this step. My brother Aharon had become a widower after his wife Esther had passed away, and my mother had moved to Kiryat Ata so she could help with the raising of his three young children. It was she, actually, who strengthened my hand in the way so typical of her – "If you believe this the right thing to do, then it is best to do as you believe."

After long deliberations, my sense of calling triumphed over all other considerations. We decided to take on the challenge and move to a frontier settlement for a period of two years. We thought two years was a logical length of time. We couldn't know that with such undertakings it is easy to determine the beginning but extremely difficult to anticipate the end.

Next came the task of choosing the destination. My initial contacts centered mainly on the northern settlement of Kiryat Shmona, which was founded in 1949 and was populated mostly by immigrants from Yemen, Persia, India and North Africa, who were later joined by immigrants from Romania and Poland.

Before we moved I made inquiries about the people living there. I also discussed the matter with Pinchas Sapir, minister of commerce and industry in those days, and Yehuda Gil, a senior member of his staff. I discovered that there was no center for technical services either in Kiryat

Shmona or for that matter in the whole area. When technical problems arose, or when they needed spare parts, the residents of Kiryat Shmona traveled all the way to Haifa or Tel Aviv. The possibility of opening up such a center enticed me, for I was a trained electronics technician and a firm believer in free enterprise. Apart from solving the problem of technical services, I thought that such a technical center would provide some relief for the growing problem of unemployment that plagued the inhabitants of the town. Any new workplace might be useful in diminishing the bitterness of the inhabitants, as well as their feelings of inferiority for having to live off seasonal farmwork offered them by the kibbutzim in the surrounding area.

After some encouraging talks with the community leaders – Mayor Asher Nizri, Chairman of the Workers Council Yitshak Shalev, and Director of the Company for the Development of Kiryat Shmona David Yaniv, the lot was cast: a center for technical services would be established in Kiryat Shmona. I also found that the education system there was in desperate need of professional teachers. Therefore, I had reason to believe that Chaya would have no problem finding a position at one of the town's schools.

The next stage for me was to try and set up a cooperative for technical services. I tried to convince technicians I knew from my former workplace at BMZA to join me in establishing the cooperative. After much persuasion I managed to conscript two young men, Yosef B., who worked in armature winding and the repair of large electrical instruments in the navy shipyard, and Gershon Levdinsky, an expert in renovating sensitive instruments in submarines. They both were about my age, married and fathers of children. We decided to establish a technical center with three departments: an electronic equipment department managed by me, an armature-winding and high-voltage electrical instrument repair department headed by Yosef, and a department for sensitive instrument renovation under Gershon.

Everything seemed to be all set, but I knew that I had to guarantee more sources of income, at least for the trial-run period. We reached an agreement with the water company Mekorot, making us responsible for running continuous checks on their water meters in the surrounding settlements, as well as maintenance on the temperature regulators in the fruit refrigerators located in the kibbutzim. We planned to perform electrical repairs and armature windings for the residents of the entire area. I assumed that we would also find some work in repairing radio receivers and amplifiers.

On paper the plans looked quite promising, but problems popped up when I came to the fundraising stage. In order to get the capital needed to start a business, I needed a loan. I spoke with the Ministry of Commerce and Industry to get authorization for a loan with low interest and no guarantors. From that moment on, our journey became long and frustrating.

I found myself running around between various government offices – of the finance, defense, commerce and industry ministries – which depleted my strength. Only later did the director of one of the ministries tell me the real reason for this: "Mr. Himmelfarb," the woman told me, "you strike us as a decent man and a patriot. However, you should know that we find it difficult to believe that a man such as you, who has obtained such a good position at so young an age, with his wife teaching in the Reali School, and you a father of two small children, would freely and willingly leave all these and move to Kiryat Shmona. We suspect that maybe you have an ulterior motive."

Finally, after exhausting efforts, a small loan without guarantors was approved by the Ministry of Commerce and Industry Fund for the Redistribution of Populace to Developmental Areas. However, it was only a small and unsatisfactory loan. We had to sell our apartment and the furniture. Chaya had to redeem the compensation she received from the school, and still we didn't have the required sum.

With the intervention of Shimon Peres, CEO of the Ministry of Defense in those days, I was given a special severance payment from the Ministry of Defense, and by authorization of the same compensation fund, we took a second loan without guarantors from the bank. Friends and family treated us as if we'd gone insane, but I believed in what I was doing. My associates, Gershon and Yosef, who like me believed in the enterprise, stood by my side and invested money from their own pockets.

We knew that at first we wouldn't see any profits, so we decided that at least in the beginning, I would move alone to Kiryat Shmona. Chaya and the children would reside temporarily in Kibbutz Gvat, and Chaya would work as a hired teacher at the kibbutz, thus covering the expense of living on the kibbutz. I would join them on weekends. My associates, Gershon and Yosef, also decided that at first they would move to Kiryat Shmona alone.

In the year 1959 we took the big step. Chaya and the children moved to Kibbutz Gvat, while I turned northward to Kiryat Shmona.

I will never forget the evening I arrived with Yosef in Kiryat Shmona. We directed the truck, loaded with equipment that we had already purchased, to the remote pavilion we had rented in the industrial district. When we arrived, we suddenly felt the air begin to whirlpool. In time we learned that in the evening hours the winds blow strongly, shaking body and soul. But that day it was a big surprise. We opened the gate to the building and began unloading equipment. Suddenly, a particularly powerful gust of wind slammed the gate doors wide open, hitting the equipment we had just unloaded. In front of our horrified eyes, several instruments were destroyed, including an expensive measuring instrument we had bought that very day. My friend Yosef's mood changed in a flash, and he immediately started yelling at me: "Where did you bring me?" he admonished me. "All the money I invested is lost! You deceived me! You told me stories of work and integration in the town, and this place we came to is Hell – I'm not staying here!" I tried to convince him that we should both stay and try to make new arrangements, but he was firm in his decision to leave. The next day he got on a truck and went back to Haifa. I never saw him again. I had to repay by myself the loans we took together, and I was very angry with him. He refused to see me, and I assume he did so because he was ashamed of himself.

I came by myself, depressed and despondent, to the apartment we rented from the Kiryat Shmona municipality. I lay on my bed and thought to myself, here I am alone in a place where I know no one, with no equipment, with heavy financial debts, and nowhere to go. I had sold my apartment in Haifa, and I was too ashamed to settle in Kibbutz Gvat. Apart from that, I was afraid that Gershon, who was scheduled to join me in a few days, would decide to leave as well after hearing about Yosef's desertion. I tried to concentrate on the motto ascribed to the heroes of Tel Hai, a phrase that was my greatest inspiration in my youth – "To take the mountain or die!" The thought somewhat strengthened me.

After a few hours I decided to go out to the only café in town. I spoke to the owner of the place, a Jew of Polish descent, and explained my troubles to him. That same evening I called Elimelech Biderman, a man with many connections in the town, and I drew some encouragement from his words. Biderman would be of great assistance to me in the future, helping me establish relations with banks, with the municipality, and with the local union. Our conversation on that first depressing night cheered me up considerably.

A few days later Gershon arrived, and to my delight, even though he knew of Yosef's departure, he decided to stay in Kiryat Shmona.

The apartment where both of us lived was quite miserable to look at, and the double bed was the main piece of furniture in it. The surrounding neighborhood suffered from filth and neglect and the local grocery shop was contaminated with cockroaches. Nevertheless, I had a pleasant surprise waiting for me: Gershon proved an idealist with left-wing views. He used to read books of philosophy and literature deep into the night, while smoking and drinking Argentinean tea from a *mate*, a container resembling a narghile. We divided the workload between ourselves and the income was put in a joint cash box. A few weeks later his wife Nurit and their two children joined us. Together we crowded into the small apartment. Nurit would wake up early each day to fix us a meal. I enjoyed hearing Gershon and Nurit speak in their undulating Spanish. Nurit joined Gershon in his work examining the water meters and she too was paid.

In my first days in town I prepared the pavilion for work. I decided to call the business Electricity and Radio Services, with the acronym of *Shachar* (literally, dawn). We didn't hang out a sign since in such a small town, the fact that we had opened our service would spread by word of mouth.

In those first months we worked very hard. It was unbearably hot inside the pavilion during the summer and extremely cold during the winter. We were afraid of the strong gusts of wind and of another dangerous door slam. Business was slow and the income meager. The residents gave me mainly broken radio sets and gramophones to fix, and they complained a great deal and asked for discounts. Inside the sets I often found cockroaches, fleas and assorted insects that crawled out when I opened them. Comparing to the advanced technology I specialized in while working in the navy, these repair jobs seemed miserably dull and boring. Occasionally I would ask myself whether this was the kind of pioneering I had come for – did I really come here to fix radio sets and release cockroaches?

Chaya and the children in Kibbutz Gvat were also going through a rough time. Chaya was charged with the education of a particularly problematic group, students the kibbutz had all but given up on. The group suffered from severe problems and great gaps were discovered among its students. Strange experiences waited for her in the classroom each day.

From the City to the Border – Seven Years in Kiryat Shmona

One day, one of the students arrived riding a donkey, and he refused to part with it under any circumstances. Other children vandalized property, but could not be reprimanded as they belonged to the kibbutz. In spite of the difficulties Chaya stood up to the task, and was greatly appreciated for it by the kibbutz members.

Chaya had to contend with the gulf between her approach to education and that of the kibbutz. In their first days at the kibbutz, nine-month-old Noam became sick and his fever rose. To alleviate his suffering Chaya took him outside for some air. As they walked on one of the paths in the kibbutz one of the children's caregivers went by and remarked, "This already makes a bad impression." Chaya was flustered by the comment, and felt insulted by the liberties strangers, and especially the caregivers – who seemed like frustrated women to her – took in giving advice about how she should raise her own children. Furthermore, the separation from four-year-old Zohar, who was forced like the rest of the kibbutz children to move to a children's house weighed on her very much. Zohar missed his mother, and suffered from being forced to eat food he didn't like. But crying and begging didn't help. The kibbutz education system back then was famous for its rigidity, and it tolerated no compromises. Eventually, as children often do, Zohar adapted and even habituated himself nicely in the company of the kibbutz children. Chaya's adaptation was much more difficult. The fact that she needed authorization for every decision she made, even pertaining to the most trivial matters, bothered her deeply. One day, when she needed margarine to bake a birthday cake for Zohar, she abstained from asking and traveled to Afula to buy it instead. All these instances strengthened her feeling that she was never meant for kibbutz life.

I visited Gvat every weekend using public transportation, which involved spending many hours on the road. Upon arrival in Gvat, I would frequently join the kibbutz members in apple picking or the gathering of crops, and I enjoyed it immensely. In time and despite Chaya's reservations, we forged beautiful bonds of friendship with some of the kibbutz members.

Later, when the time came to leave the kibbutz, people insisted that we join as members, and even offered to settle all our loans for us if we stayed with them. The offer was both flattering and tempting, but I knew that if I were to give in to the temptation I would feel like I had failed in my original mission. I would also feel that I had abused the kibbutz's kindness. We decided to continue with the original plan. We separated on good terms with the members of Kibbutz Gvat, and in later years we occasionally returned for visits.

All this happened after one year. Throughout that long year I waited impatiently for Chaya and the children to join me. My mother would chide me repeatedly: "A responsible man doesn't leave his wife in the kibbutz and drive off to search for work." Her words affected me, and I felt that leaving Chaya and the kids alone was not a decent thing to do.

I commenced preparations for my family's expected return. I vacated the apartment where I had lived for a year with Gershon and his family, and moved to my own apartment in Housing Complex D. It included two bedrooms and a living room, but it looked quite shabby. Chaya was appalled when she first saw it, but she took solace in the view from the window, which included beautiful green expanses and the peak of Mount Hermon.

We found it difficult to get used to to the northern weather, especially to the damage caused by the afternoon gales. One day the wind blew in and destroyed a beautiful crystal vase that we both loved. But I think the true shock was cultural. We were amazed to see people throw garbage from the windows into the street. We found it difficult to believe that people would walk to the butcher with their chicken in their hands, plucking its feathers all along the way. We saw parents wearing fur coats, with their children trudging barefoot by them. We had difficulties believing stories of immigrants pickling cucumbers in toilets. Nevertheless, we did like the warm-hearted simple people, with their Zionist-Messianic ideology and their willingness to make great personal sacrifices for the sake of striking roots in the land.

Chaya began teaching in the elementary school Metzudot, which had especially large classes. She saw her work as a true calling, and it provided her with both challenges and fulfillment. She accompanied one class for a few years and managed to advance it considerably. Afterwards she educated other classes and was always very successful in her duties. Furthermore, toward the end of our stay in the town she was even offered the position of principal of the school. Chaya declined, among other reasons because she wished to continue teaching and not deal only with management and bureaucratic issues. In addition to her regular schedule she instructed soldier-teachers who came after a short military course to fill the incredible shortage of teachers. She took them under her wing, and devoted to

From the City to the Border – Seven Years in Kiryat Shmona 101

them many hours of her own time.

Zohar and Noam were sent to a kindergarten under the care of the excellent kindergarten teacher Miryam Raiskin, the wife of Yosef Raiskin-Edin, who managed the Company for the Development of Kiryat Shmona. Afterwards, when the children were a bit older, they attended the Metzudot school. Even though there were mental gulfs to bridge, our sons got along well with the children there.

In those days Kiryat Shmona was suffering from severe economic and social difficulties, in addition to security concerns. First and foremost the settlement had a serious shortage of places to work. The surrounding kibbutzim had established a few factories, mainly to provide employment for the residents of the town, but this was not enough. Factories, a central bakery and the major auto-repair shop of Upper Galilee, as well as the seasonal farmwork in the kibbutzim, did not create enough permanent places of work to alleviate the economic distress.

The town was in trouble on the social front as well. A lot of tension existed between the immigrants from Middle Eastern countries and the immigrants from Poland and Romania. The latter had come to live in the town upon its establishment, but were now preparing to leave. Furthermore, many of the young folk who during their military service were exposed to new professions, new possibilities of life or a new boyfriend or girlfriend, moved elsewhere permanently. Moreover, the poor level of education, the inadequate health services and the lack of any recreational possibilities did not add to the town's attractiveness.

As if this were not enough, the area suffered from security troubles. The Katyusha barrages began only years later, but Feddayun infiltrators from refugee camps in Lebanon used to harass the residents. Several times they broke into farms in the area, stealing property and livestock, and sometimes they even attacked people traveling the roads, wounding or taking over their vehicles. Apart from this, the Syrians in the Golan continued to bombard valley settlements along the border, and Tel Kazir, Shamir and Dan suffered from repeated bombardments. Most of the conflicts erupted over the diversion of the water line, and once in a while air battles were conducted between Israeli and Syrian aircrafts. In one of the battles two enemy crafts were shot down into the Sea of Galilee.

Life in Kiryat Shmona was not kind to its inhabitants. I knew I had acted for the good of my country by moving with my family to a northern town, especially now that many of its citizens were abandoning it, but I felt that I needed to do more. And I knew exactly where to start.

As a member of the Mapai party I was chosen to head the party office in the town, and I began to integrate myself in its activities and its social involvement. First and foremost I made a goal of bringing together the immigrants and the kibbutz people. I started with "trivialities." I organized integrated public sing-alongs and soccer and volleyball games for the kibbutz young people and the immigrants. Many kibbutzniks, some of them famous public figures, lent a hand and helped me. Among them were Ehud Avriel from Naot Mordechai, Natan Cohen and Joe Creiden from Kfar Blum and Grisha from Kfar Giladi, who have all since passed away. Through my membership in the Mapai Party I befriended Saadia Galev from Kfar Blum and David Yaniv from Naot Mordechai, may they live long lives, and they too lent their assistance.

In the year 1960 I helped establish the Rotary Club. The initiator was Doctor Ruben Katthein, the head veterinary of the area and a citizen of Kiryat Shmona, who was acquainted with the club from the United States. He invited me to take part in the foundation of the local club. We assembled more members and arrived at the number necessary for the club's formation. The most meaningful project we set in motion at the beginning was a "House for Soldier Teachers," under the auspices of which we adopted the female soldiers serving as teachers in Kiryat Shmona, hosting them on Saturdays and arranging various cultural activities for them. We also initiated Operation "Respect Your Elders." At our request, the Egged Bus Cooperative gave us buses for the town's elderly and we took them on a trip in the flowering Galilee. For many of them it was their first excursion in the area, and to our delight they enjoyed every minute of it.

We planned and executed many other projects, including gathering clothes in Tel Aviv and distributing them to the town's needy, supplying heaters to the elderly in winter and inviting speakers from the center of the country to give lectures on various subjects. We established the Education Encouragement Fund which gave high school scholarships to the community's youth. The various activities were financed with inheritance funds, club membership fees, private contributions and donations from organizations such as Solel Boneh (Israel's largest construction and infrastructure-contracting company). In addition, we initiated youth exchanges with members abroad.

We thus developed an autonomous system of community service that was independent of factional political parties. I enjoyed my activities with the club immensely, and I found great satisfaction from the help we were able to give to the public.

At the end of 1960, with the help of a few friends, I established the Artisans' Association. I believed in the importance of private enterprise and in supporting individuals' ambitions for economic independence. The organization endeavored to protect the interests of the small artisans – locksmiths and shopkeepers and the like – who had no public representation.

I took it upon myself to head the organization, and took care of matters such as taxes, legal aid and other problems that eventually arose. I conducted disputes with the various municipalities and the Bureau of Commerce and Industry in Tel Aviv. Among other things I managed to wrest from the income-tax authorities approval for decreased tax payments in developmental areas and discounts in municipal property taxes. In 1963, the price-index method was introduced and the Rasco Company informed all business owners in the commercial centers that rents would be attached to the price index from now on. I tried to fight this harmful decree by announcing a strike, but I did not succeed. Rasco didn't grant our request, and in the end, we had to pay index-attached rent. As chairman of the organization I also approached members of the surrounding kibbutzim and persuaded them to use the services of artisans from Kiryat Shmona. These measures had significant implications for the owners of small and new businesses in town.

In those days there was no institute for technological education in operation. As a believer in the significance of education generally and technological education specifically, I felt it would be appropriate to bring technological education to the town. Since I was an electronics instructor, I decided to give lectures to the town's teenagers. For a few months I gave lectures on the subjects of electricity and radio in city hall. I taught a group of ten to twelve students, teaching them such basics as the operation of radio tubes and how we receive radio waves.

By this time the workshop was growing and I was in need of an assistant, and at the same time I was asked by the staff of the welfare department to help train problematic immigrant youth in the technological professions. They suggested I take several of them under my wing and train them in those areas. I was promised that the welfare department would pay the lion's share of their salary. I agreed therefore to take two or three of the many youths who were referred to me as aides. It was not a simple experience. It turned out that most of them hadn't even finished elementary school. They came from Russian homes, suffered from health maladies and for the most part showed no interest in the studies, finding it difficult to comprehend even the simplest subjects I taught. Some of them even caused damage when they broke or burned equipment. Over and over again I would notice that batteries, records and other items were missing.

Nevertheless, their short training under me qualified them for conscription to the Ordinance and Communications Corps, and in most cases they were sent to courses and qualified as technicians. This fact gave me great satisfaction. After their military service, regrettably, they did not return to Kiryat Shmona, and chose for the most part to stay in the central region of the country. This choice didn't allow me to make use of them and the knowledge they accumulated in the IDF, and the town did not benefit from them or their skills.

Only in one case was I allowed to taste the fruits of my efforts. Lucian Gal, a very talented young man, actually began working for me after his military service in a technical position. His talents showed immediately and he was really able to help me. It was to Lucian and another person to whom, much later, I would sell my business.

After working in repairs for two years without having managed to advance economically, I decided to try my luck at selling electrical appliances. I purchased gramophones, radio sets, cooking stoves, washing machines, refrigerators and other appliances from major distributors on credit and put them on sale. In those days prices weren't supervised, but were determined by supply and demand. I matched my prices to the very limited economic capabilities of townspeople and kibbutz members in the area. Sometimes I even sold the merchandise with credit payments and large discounts, such that I would make only a small profit or at times none at all.

During that year I also began marketing television sets, which had just started appearing in the country. Although television broadcasts began only several years later, reception of Lebanese broadcasts was possible in the north, and the people of Kiryat Shmona, many of whom spoke Arabic, desired to purchase the wonder-device. I ordered a certain quantity of black-and-white sets, and through local sub-contractors we installed tower-mounted antennas which enabled broadcast reception from Lebanon.

We were soon plagued by many technical problems. Apparently the distributor had unknowingly received second-hands sets, and their quality was poor. The powerful winds in the area often knocked down the antennas, which caused disruptions in reception and constituted a serious safety hazard. In addition, television reception was often interrupted by a phenomenon called "reflex." The broadcast waves coming from Lebanon were broken up on a few mountains in the area, causing the screen to show two or three silhouettes superimposed one upon the other. The local residents found it hard to believe we were dealing with a physical phenomenon resulting from the nature of wave dispersion. A few even believed it was the doing of a higher power, and in most cases I could not convince them otherwise.

One day one of my clients' sons fell from a scaffolding and was seriously wounded. His family believed the demons from the Lebanese television were responsible.

I'll never forget how I was invited to exorcise the "demons" from the television set. In the entrance I was greeted by four large pictures that were displayed in most of the Persian residents' homes: the picture of Queen Suraya who was much beloved by Jews of Persian birth, the Persian Shah, the picture of the Rambam and the picture of Rabbi Shimon Bar Yochai. When I entered the living room I saw the community rabbi sitting in front of the television and splashing the screen with assorted liquids while mumbling spells and enchantments. All the family members sat around him and prayed. I feared the retaliation of the household but luckily nothing happened. In this occasion, as in others, I endeavored to repair the malfunction using the tools and technical knowledge I had at my disposal and fortunately I succeeded in the task.

With the initiative of radio manufacturers from Tel Aviv and Haifa, I one day announced a trade-in sale. Anyone who brought in his old radio set or tape recorder could buy a new one at a large discount. Many residents jumped at the opportunity, especially people from the kibbutzim, who arrived in pickup trucks loaded with dozens of old instruments. Soon my workshop was filled with old sets that I had no need for. At first I shipped them to Tel Aviv, but the warehouse workers there soon informed me that they had no room to store the appliances coming in from all over the country, and that we should stop sending them. We had no choice but to load a tractor with all the appliances and dispose of them in the municipal garbage dump.

Meanwhile, my loyal associate, Gershon Levdinsky, decided he had no interest in the sales business, and wanted to terminate our partnership. We separated as friends, and I was left alone to run the business. Gershon and his wife remained in town and continued to make a living from the repair of water meters and other instruments – mainly temperature regulators for fruit refrigerators, a field that had developed greatly in Galilee.

Despite plentiful work, I was for various reasons not satisfied with the development of the business, and so I became a silent partner with Elimelech Biderman, a highly respected property owner, in the ownership of two movie houses. We tried to expand, but we didn't make enough profits. A few years later, before I left Kiryat Shmona, I quit this field as well and sold my shares to the Goldberg family from Metulah. (The late Yossi Goldberg presided for many years as Metulah's mayor). The theaters continued to function a few more years before it was decided to convert them into real-estate property.

I tried my hand in selling records as well. In Kiryat Shmona there was a great demand for records. Oriental, Turkish and Indian music were especially popular. Their fame came from the movies that were screened in the local cinema, which were very popular among the local residents. Many of the town's residents yearned to buy the recorded soundtracks of the films, which usually included romantic, melodious love songs. They also loved eastern music hits, like those of Joe Amar and Avi Toledano, who were very popular at that time. Other clients were looking for records by western singers such as Paul Anka, Cliff Richards, Joan Baez, Italian singers and French chanson singers. Kibbutz members, in contrast, preferred to buy records of modern Hebrew songs.

Many people bought records, but this never succeeded in making me rich. Headaches, on the other hand, were supplied profusely.

Occasionally Chaya would help me with sales. One day I drove to Tel Aviv, leaving Chaya alone in the store. Chaya, who had advised me to get rid of all the records in the store since they caused more trouble than they're worth, decided to announce a sale. She sold most of the records in the store at a reduced price, for even less than their original cost, to Indian immigrant customers who crowded around the store in droves. Hundreds of records were sold at once, and since then entire groups of Indian immigrants used to visit the store and ask me: "Mr. Dawid, when will the lady arrive?" No matter what answer I gave, they waited long hours for her with their characteristically endless patience but Chaya never returned to the store.

The great efforts I invested in my work and the various public projects I participated in took a toll on my health. I suffered from digestive problems. They had originally appeared during the period of the Holocaust but were now getting worse. The health services in town weren't of serious quality, so I traveled to hospitals in Safed or Haifa for various treatments.

The trips to Safed, Haifa and Tel Aviv were made with the family car, a small second-hand Renault 4 which frequently broke down. I had specifically chosen this modest car, which I bought in 1960, to keep people from becoming jealous. In one of our family trips I discovered that the breaks were inoperative, and it was only through sheer luck that we didn't have an accident. The car also served me when I drove along the border to my friend from Kibbutz Gvat, the late Eliezer Barkin. Barkin served as a liaison officer to the United Nations during his reserve duty. Every time I visited Eliezer, I brought him to my house for a shower and a decent meal, returning him afterwards to his base. These drives were jeopardous, not only because of the car's ramshackle condition – Barkin was stationed in a Syrian area manned by the United Nations. The roads were in a poor state, and the Renault gave me a lot of trouble. Luckily I never ran into any Syrians, and the trips concluded safely.

A few years later, in 1964, we decided to turn in the old Renault for a simple Mini-Minor which we bought for modesty's sake. The salesman assured me that it was a strong, reliable car, and even the Queen Mother and Princess Elizabeth rode in a car of this model. But apparently the respectable ladies of court never drove on the roads ascending to Kiryat Shmona. At any rate, even this car overheated at times while climbing the roads to town, and occasionally I had to stop and wait for the engine to cool.

In 1962 we moved to a neighborhood of double-story cottages. The town's wealthier residents lived in this neighborhood. In our new and spacious home we would entertain family members from all over the country - my brother Aharon, who in the meantime had married his second wife Deborah, my brother Yosef, of blessed memory, and his family and of course my mother, of blessed memory. They all honored the Sabbath and the holidays, and therefore usually arrived in the intermediate days of Sukkot and Passover.

Chaya and I became quite well known and appreciated in the town. The adults knew me as the "Repair Man" and the children knew me mainly as "*Morah* (Teacher) Chaya's husband." One day I was spotted by one of the residents while washing my car and he told me: "In Casablanca it is not dignified for a great merchant, a famous man such as yourself, to wash his car. It is humiliating for us…," and he begged me to let him do it for me. Obviously I declined politely but firmly. As was our way, we tried to keep a modest lifestyle and were careful not to arouse jealousy in our fellow citizens.

One day I was hired to install a loudspeaker system at the school where Chaya taught. When I arrived I bumped into the school principal. "Listen," he said, looking a bit perplexed, "Three teachers called in sick today, and now I have three classes without teachers. Since you are Chaya's husband, the best and most devoted teacher in the school, I assume that you too are as educated as she, so I beg of you, do me a favor, go into one of the classes and give them a lesson on any subject you wish – electricity, the Bible, anything – and the loudspeaker system can wait till tomorrow." I had some reservations, but the principal wouldn't take no for an answer. In the classroom, I explained to the children how a loudspeaker system works and I told them about airwaves and electrical waves and other such matters. The children were very interested in the new and exciting material, and the principal was very grateful.

During our stay in Kiryat Shmona we formed many diverse social relationships. Older married people, bachelors and young couples were all part of our social circle. Despite the hard work and the financial concerns, we enjoyed a busy and satisfying social and spiritual life.

In the beginning of 1962 I decided to move the business to a more central location, and I chose Resko – the commercial center of the town. I invested in the store's design, hiring the service of an architect from Safed, and together we designed a special décor. On one of the walls we placed a world map, a symbol of communication. We built a bar and tall benches, so the customers could sit, listen to music and enjoy a cup of coffee. In the intersection near the entrance to town we hung a big sign with the business's name, Radio Shachar, lit with neon lights. These kinds of signs were yet to be seen in a northern town.

I invested a small fortune in the store's new home. The townspeople were impressed by the place, and sales were to my satisfaction. But in the beginning of 1963 a terrible incident occurred. One night a fire broke out in the store. The neighbors called the fire department, but the sprays of water and foam did worse damage than the actual fire. A sizeable portion of the store's contents were destroyed. After the "plague of wind" that I had suffered on my first day in Kiryat Shmona, I was now struck with a "plague of fire." Some people thought that the place had caught fire from a spark flying out of one of the transformers, while others suspected foul play by commercial rivals.

In 1964 I advertised another sale of 250 used car radios of American manufacture, and installed them in the trucks and heavy vehicles of the Upper Galilee shipping companies. After the installation there were many problems. The ignition process of these vehicles created vibrations that harmed many of the sets. Furthermore, the trucks used unpaved roads, and the violent shaking either damaged the sets or caused noise. The car radios were not of high quality. Again I had created an unnecessary headache for myself.

A real change in my career took place at this time. Yosef Raiskin-Edin, director of the Company for the Development of Kiryat Shmona, resigned, and I was asked to take his place. I had to make a difficult decision. I used to visit my mother, who lived alone in Kiryat Ata and whose health was deteriorating, once a week. Each visit she would warn me not to accumulate too many assets, and chided me with the famous aphorism: "The more possessions, the more worry." I thought about it for a while, and finally decided I would accept the offer. In 1964 I quit the business I had built with my own hands, the business that had endured so many trials and tribulations across the years, and sold it to two of my employees: Lucian Gal, who had completed his studies while working in my shop and who showed marvelous technical skill, and Moshe Avshalom, a resident of Kiryat Shmona.

In my new post I had to work toward the establishment of new factories and the creation of workplaces by transferring factories from central Israel, as well as initiate and carry out various other projects.

As a result of my worldview and the difficult financial state in the town and company, I refused to accept an executive's vehicle from the company. I continued driving my small Morris to Tel Aviv and Jerusalem for the company's affairs, and received reimbursement only for direct expenses. The funding for the company came from government loans, bank loans and investments of well-established companies like Solel Boneh and the Workers' Company of the Histadrut, as well as from wealthy private investors.

At times, there were conflicts of interest. The investors were interested in quickly accumulating profits from their investments, while I put the public interest at the top of my priorities. Therefore I often felt that I was letting my friends down, as well as people who trusted me enough to invest in local projects. Most of the Board of Directors was composed of Solel Boneh executives, and I pressured them to direct the company's funds into public projects in spite of financial uncertainties.

Matters advanced slowly. We completed the construction of the Hatzafon Hotel and the Snir Cinema – projects that had commenced during my predecessor's days. A contractor who was actually our subsidiary built both structures. Elimelech Biderman, who was also the main shareholder, managed it. We also established a sewing workshop in town, which employed thirty workers at its peak, and a diamond polishing plant belonging to an entrepreneur from Tel Aviv.

These businesses eventually failed, mainly as a result of their distance from industry centers and the expensive salaries demanded by specialists who were brought from afar.

The tourism potential of Upper Galilee, which was a green, beautiful region with abundant water, had not yet been utilized. In order to stir up the tourist industry in the area I made a suggestion that seemed very novel, if not revolutionary, at the time – the construction of a cable railway from Kibbutz Menara, through Kiryat Shmona, to the Dan water springs, with a stop at the Tel Hai historical site. I thought and hoped the idea would excite the Board of Directors and generate a real change in Kiryat Shmona's financial situation. I made a great effort to advance the project. I made use of Yosef Cohen, my cousin and the Haifa city engineer, who was building the Carmelit, Haifa's subway, at the time. But to my great disappointment, the Company for Development's Board of Directors had misgivings. The expenditure seemed too great to them. They thought it would be a better idea to make a concentrated effort and direct the meager resources to a goal of creating short-term workplaces. Because of this very original idea I gained the nickname of "Visionary," but the idea itself was eventually shelved, or at least postponed. From time to time, especially during elections, the idea was brought up again, and a variety of candidates used it as a campaign gimmick. Employees from different institutions followed the "Cable Railway" idea abroad, mainly to Switzerland, to learn how to build cable railways and also to try and find investors. Finally, in 1997, the idea became a reality.

A Swiss company established a cable railway between Kibbutz Menara and Kiryat Shmona. The founders, the administration and the people of Menara ignored the "pioneers" of the idea and I wasn't even invited to the opening, but the satisfaction for coming up with the original initiative is something no one can take from me.

In November 1964 our youngest son was born. We called him Lior, because he was born close to the Hanukkah holiday, and we added the name Zvi in memory of my late brother Hershel (*zvi* and *hersh* are Hebrew and Yiddish for "deer"). Unlike many of our friends, who drove to Safed, Haifa or even Tel Aviv for the birth, Chaya and I decided that the baby would burst forth into the air of this world in the maternity clinic in Kiryat Shmona. When Chaya came to give birth in the miserable hut that served as the local maternity clinic, there was no doctor there at all, and we had to call him from his home. In later days Lior, now a family man himself, would boast that on his birth certificate is written: "born in Kiryat Shmona."

I didn't have enough time during the week to spend with my children, and the burden of raising them fell on Chaya's shoulders. When she was asked to become the principal of Mezudot school she declined, since she preferred to devote her time to taking care of our children. Nevertheless, she did not approve of me spending too much time in my public endeavors, while our own financial situation and quality of life remained low, and the children's education left much to be desired.

Still, the main reason I decided to leave was political. In 1966 the Labor Party split when Ben-Gurion, Shimon Peres, Teddy Kollak, Almogi, Yitshak Navon, Moshe Dayan and Ehud Avriel established the Rafi movement, going against Labor party veterans Golda Meir, Levi Eshkol and Pinchas Sapir. Repercussions from this split reached all the way up north. Rafi politicians rounded up support in town, and Shimon Peres came several times to Kiryat Shmona, winning the hearts of its residents with his speeches. He told them they wouldn't be menial workers anymore, promising them "a car for every worker."

His words encouraged the townspeople, but put us public servants in a tough position. As the Rafi movement's influence in town strengthened, I felt, as a Mapai man, that my status was being compromised. The kibbutz people in the area also supported Rafi and they saw me as a man of the old establishment, resulting in strained relations between us.

Moreover, incitement of an ethnic nature was rife in the city. The mayor Asher Nizri accused me, as well as the rest of Mapai's supporters, of acting in a patronizing manner toward the new immigrants. It angered him that I was appointed Director of the Company for Development of Kiryat Shmona, while I was no more than a small business owner. He maintained that I was appointed because I was a Mapai man. It should be noted that my friend David Morre, who emigrated from Iraq and succeeded Nizri as mayor, supported me instead of him. David Morre succeeded me in my position as Director of the Company for Development upon my resignation and subsequent departure from Kiryat Shmona.

At the end of 1966, seven years after we moved to Kiryat Shmona instead of the two years we had originally planned, we left the town. Seven years is not something to be trifled with. It is a large slice of our life. This time in my own and my family's life, with all its ordeals, had great significance. I know that Chaya and I contributed to the settlement of Kiryat Shmona in many ways – publicly, economically, culturally and socially. Moreover, we were enriched with many experiences. We were exposed to a different way of life than we were used to, and we acquired quite a few good friends.

Today I can admit that I made a few mistakes, and I had to pay dearly. Unlike my friends in Tel Aviv and Haifa, I hardly advanced professionally. Furthermore, the value of my friends' apartments doubled several time over, while I could sell my house in Kiryat Shmona after ten years only at a very low price. The many Katyushas that fell on the town were the main cause of the house's low economic value. In the public arena I didn't make any meaningful advance either, mainly because I operated on the level of implementation rather than as a supervisor. I was more of a naïve idealist than a politician.

Many years after our departure I still suffered the consequences of the move to Kiryat Shmona, since my years working as an independent businessman did not count toward my pension. Chaya's career also tread water, while her colleagues progressed noticeably.

Despite all of these considerations I do not regret the years we spent in Kiryat Shmona. I think it made a significant contribution to the country, and I am grateful to Chaya for supporting me and helping me fulfill my ideological aspirations. Despite all the difficulties she always stood by my side.

CHAPTER EIGHT

Joining the Defense Industry

The years in Kiryat Shmona, despite their moral value, constituted from a financial point of view an unsuccessful adventure, if not a failure. The Katyushas that were fired at the northern town every now and then frustrated the sale of the apartment, leaving us with little means of affording a new apartment elsewhere. A house serves as an anchor and security for a person, a place from which he can leave and to which he can return. Therefore we decided to make every effort to buy a house despite the financial difficulties it involved. Returning to Haifa seemed a logical decision, and with Chaya's encouragement we bought an apartment that was still being built in the French Carmel area.

Next came the challenge of finding a job. My friend Lieutenant Colonel Ephraim Talmon, who at the time served as the contact man between the navy and the Israel Aircraft Industries (IAI, currently Israel Aerospace Industries), told me about the project for the production of the sea-to-sea missile Gabriel. He suggested that I check out the possibility of joining the project which was being implemented at the IAI in the middle of the country. At this stage it was clear to me that the possibilities of finding work in the center of Israel were better, so that we would be wise to move our residence to the greater Tel Aviv area. We rented out the apartment in Haifa and rented a house for ourselves in the Zahala neighborhood of

Tel Aviv. It was one of those one-story old houses that were built in the '50s for commissioned army officers. Our neighbors Chedva and Yehuda Segev helped us greatly in settling in to Zahala, and we became close friends.

Even though Ephraim's suggestion was appealing, I did not hurry to look into it. After years of being the independent owner of my own business I hesitated to return to being a salaried employee. In addition, I was afraid of getting into much more advanced and complex technology after years of being cut off from these advances by my long stay in Kiryat Shmona. Therefore I chose in the meantime to work at a Tel Aviv company that marketed electrical parts, which in time I planned to become a partner of. But the work was not challenging for me, and after a few months I resigned and got in touch with the IAI. I advanced through the accepted stages of the Employment Bureau, and after a rather long time during which I passed a series of security checks, I was accepted for work at the IAI.

At the end of 1966 I began to work at Mabat (Plant B) in Yehud where the Gabriel missile project was being implemented. The name of the company was suggested by the poet Natan Alterman in response to a request by Elhanan Yishai, the deputy manager of the company who later became its general manager. The company was founded and managed by Ori Eventov, the son of the first secretary of the Knesset, Mrs. Hanna Eventov.

The transfer to a new environment, although done freely, was not at all easy for my family and myself. We did not expect any medals for our stay in Kiryat Shmona, but we also didn't expect the reserved attitude which we encountered.

During the first months Chaya had difficulty in finding work. The depression had already begun in Israel and the Ministry of Education told her that they first had to worry about their veteran teachers. Chaya tried to explain that for six years she was a teacher for the children of Kiryat Shmona as part of a directed policy of the government but her words fell on deaf ears. "We in the Ministry of Education didn't send you there." Eventually Chaya found work as a teacher in a school in Ramat HaChayal and as a substitute teacher in Maoz Aviv. Later on she joined the staff of the elementary school Elharizi in Tel Baruch as a tenured teacher.

My two oldest sons Zohar and Noam didn't have an easy time either. They started to study at the local school in Zahala. They filled in the gaps in their studies relatively easily but from a social standpoint they ran into problems. Zohar and Noam knew that the years in Kiryat Shmona were spent volunteering for the good of the state and they were surprised and hurt by the denigrating attitude toward "the Second Israel."

As a result of these considerations we decided at the end of 1968, after two years in Zahala, to leave the neighborhood and move to Ramat Gan. In order to buy an apartment in the city we had to sell our apartment in Haifa and Kiryat Shmona, although the depression that was still present in Israel made it difficult for us to sell. After much effort we finally managed to sell the two apartments, and with the money we bought an apartment in Tel Ganim in Ramat Gan. It was a very nice apartment in a quiet and cultured neighborhood drowned in greenery which was built at the beginning of the '50s. The children loved the house and the neighborhood and in a short time acquired friends. The modest, middle-class atmosphere in Ramat Gan suited us all. Chaya and I loved the tranquility and pleasant atmosphere of the neighborhood and we continued to live in the same apartment for the next twenty-six years, until 1994.

In the meantime, although I began to work at Mabat with great enthusiasm, I discovered fairly quickly that the technological advancement that had occurred since I had left the field in 1958 was greater than I had imagined. Ori Eventov developed the idea of a unique device, the first of its kind in the world. This device converted the Gabriel missile into a "skimmer," meaning that before hitting its target the missile flew about five feet above the wavy surface of the sea. This assured an effective hit of the target. Ephraim, who represented the customer, made sure that the missile's performance matched the requirements set by the navy. I felt that I had entered a different world which was run by young, competent, and knowledgeable engineers. I understood that I had to close this gap quickly. Filled with the challenge of proving that I still had it in me, I immediately applied for practical and theoretical studies. I registered for professional courses in navigation and guidance systems, and joined the evening lessons at the Management School (now The Management College) on Allenby Road in Tel Aviv.

Despite the difficulties of getting acclimated I enjoyed working at the IAI. The ideas and prejudices I had held about the field fell apart. I learned that dealing with the technological professions, which I had always considered uninteresting, was actually filled with Zionism in the best meaning of the word. At the company there was an atmosphere of competitive enthusiasm and an ambition to succeed. Efforts were made to complete the project as quickly as possible without compromising on accuracy and reliability. Ori Eventov, the man of vision, and his team tried to prove to the management of the Ministry of Defense that their choice of Mabat was a correct one. We did everything possible to keep on schedule and to stay within the available budget.

Work at the company was carried on under conditions of high pressure. The winds of war began to blow in our area, and the Ministry of Defense and the navy demanded the completion of the missile development project. After the sinking of the destroyer *Eilat* by the Kummar missile of Egypt on October 1967 the navy put more pressure on us to finish the project quickly. During that catastrophe forty-seven sailors were killed and ninety-one wounded. Almost on a daily basis we were required to remain at the plant until ten at night. My health deteriorated, and I began to suffer again from problems in my digestive and nervous systems. My family life, too, suffered from this exhausting race. Most of my energy was devoted to my professional work and little to my children. As in the days of Kiryat Shmona, most of the burden fell again on Chaya's shoulders. I was well regarded at work and was given a promotion, but the price I paid in my personal and family life was too high.

Despite the pressure and the high professional standards, work at the plant was carried on in an almost kibbutz-like atmosphere. Engineers and technicians walked around the plant in shorts and sandals, and called one another by their nicknames. And yet the creative tension was thick enough to be cut with a knife. Most of those involved in the project worked day and night for the project's success without any compensation for their many hours of overtime. Their fulfillment came from the success of the project.

The missile's first test took place on October 8, 1973, during the Yom Kippur War in the Nile Delta. Thirteen Egyptian and Syrian missile boats were sunk by Gabriel missiles while the Israeli navy suffered no losses. The happiness of the navy and our team at Mabat knew no bounds. Team pride expanded unbelievably. The loud cry of "We did it!" was heard throughout the plant. After the extraordinary success of the Gabriel missile it became an international weapon. In time Ori Eventov was awarded the Israeli Defense Prize for his development and supervision of the project.

In 1969 I was charged with collecting the technical documentation of the Gabriel project, including documentation of the whole system and its parts, as well as the maintenance of the missiles. The massive amount of documentation had accumulated in a number of languages – Hebrew, English and Italian – but the Israeli navy required that the literature conform to international standards in Hebrew and English. Italy was then a supplier of weapons to the Israeli navy. During the War of Independence Israel made use of "Little Pigs" – small, one-person sabotage boats made in Italy. And when the modernization phase began in the navy, it was helped by Italian know-how. For the first missile boats many subunits and accessories made in Italy were used until we acquired the know-how to produce them in Israel. For the job of documentation to which I was appointed I registered for a course in Italian at the Berlitz Language School, which was sponsored by the plant. At the same time I continued my certificate course in business management at the Management College, and for this devoted two evenings a week for two years.

In my position as head of the technical documentation department, I was allowed to shape the unit as I wanted. Slowly I built a documentation department of twelve members which included graphic artists, writers, draftsmen and engineers.

As I progressed with the cataloging it became evident that the terminology that was used by the Italians was not sufficiently clear to us. In order to clarify problems and improve communication between us I was sent for a few weeks to Italy. I visited the plants of three main companies. The largest of them was Galileo, in Florence, which produced optical systems for civilian and military use. The company was called after the Italian scientist Galileo Galilei, and numbered the Italian navy among its clients. I also visited two branches of the Selenia Company, in Rome and Naples, which specialized in the production of radar systems.

In the coastal city of La Spezia I visited a third company, Oto Melara, which produced naval guns. La Spezia was known over the years as having great strategic importance. During World War II the Germans used the city as a naval base, and submarines would be dispatched from there to attack British ships. At the end of the war she served as a base point for the activities of the Zionist illegal immigration and many ships sailed from her port to the coast of Palestine. To this day there is a sign in Hebrew which reads *Shaarei Zion*. At the various plants I met Italian technicians and despite our broken English we succeeded in understanding one another and I was able to carry out my mission.

After I completed putting together the literature on the Gabriel I took time off to instruct various groups of the IAI and navy on how to use the literature, and I enjoyed this very much. I suppose that I was the only soldier in Zahal who during the War of Attrition received an emergency call-up for service in Florence. I stayed in Italy at that time for two weeks.

In 1971 the army representative in Rome, Zvi Alon, suggested that I be sent to Rome for a longer period of time as supervisor of the relations between Mabat and the various plants producing naval weapons in Italy. He also wanted me to be in charge of supervising the various teams of the navy active in Italy. The General Manager of Mabat, Elhanan Yishai, asked me to accept the job and I decided to accept the challenge.

Throughout this time Chaya had continued to teach at the Elharizi School. Zohar, who showed an aptitude for technical subjects, was studying electronics at ORT. He worked very hard and in time became one of the school's outstanding students. Noam studied at the Herzliya Gymnasia for high school.

The decision to move to Italy naturally affected all the family members. Chaya was happy at the opportunity of traveling to Italy. We decided to take Noam and Lior with us while Zohar, our oldest, remained in Israel because the time for his matriculation examinations was approaching. We planned to go for one year. We found a temporary home for Zohar close to the home of his friend Gadi and they studied together for the exams. We maintained close contact with him during the entire time of our stay in Italy. In 1972 Zohar registered for studies toward a BSc degree in Electrical Engineering at the Technion – the only one of his class to be accepted as a pre-army student. He went to live in the dormitories there and during his vacation fulfilled his obligations to the army, finished boot camp and completed the officer's course.

As was common in those days, for my trip as an official representative of the Ministry of Defense, I was asked to change my family name from Himmelfarb (*the color of the heavens*, in Yiddish) to a name of Hebrew origin. I chose the name Shachar (*dawn*, in Hebrew) since its meaning was close to the original family name and also because I had used this name in the past during my days in Kiryat Shmona.

CHAPTER NINE

My First Assignment in Italy

In July 1971 Chaya and I arrived with Naom and Lior in Rome. We searched for an apartment in the center of town, from which we could easily get around the city, and which would be as close as possible to the Israeli Embassy. The apartment on Via Flaminia 213 met our needs and during the summer months we lived comfortably in our new residence. However, in September, the time that most of Rome's residents return from their vacations, we discovered how wrong we had been. The apartment stood on a major traffic route leading to the center of Rome, and tens of thousands of cars used it daily, deafening our ears with their relentless noise. Furthermore, the window panes of our apartment accumulated soot daily from the exhaust pipes of passing cars.

One day Lior saw a bird chirping outside the window. "Mom," cried the seven-year-old child, "What's this? Did they give that bird an exhaust pipe instead of a beak?" In spite of this we remained in the apartment, both because of its convenient location and because I was too preoccupied with my work to look for a new one. About a year and a half later we moved to a different apartment in a quieter, calmer area, Via Ronciglione, in northern Rome. We lived there for four years, until the end of our stay in Italy.

Chaya and the children took to Rome easily and had no trouble settling in. A short time after our arrival Chaya signed up for Italian ern Rome. We lived there for four years, until the end of our stay in Italy.

Chaya and the children took to Rome easily and had no trouble settling in. A short time after our arrival Chaya signed up for Italian Language and Art studies at the Dante Alighieri school, which belonged to a worldwide chain of schools devoted to teaching Italian culture. In time she collaborated with another Israeli teacher in organizing private Hebrew lessons for all the Israeli children. The lessons were encouraged by the Ministry of Foreign Affairs and funded by the Israeli Embassy, since in those days there was no Hebrew school system in place. The initiative of the two women helped the children adapt to their schools when they returned to Israel.

At first we sent our children to study in the American School, in which the classes were conducted in a casual and pleasant manner, and the social atmosphere was also inviting. Later we transferred Noam to the English St. Georges High School. His diploma from St. Georges was recognized by the Israeli Ministry of Education and enabled him to sign up for higher education in Israel. For Lior we found a private Hebrew teacher, since we were afraid he would forget his mother tongue.

I soon realized that my knowledge of Italian was unsatisfactory. I began studying Italian with Fosca Freda, the sister of our landlord from Via Flaminia. My Italian gradually improved, to the point that I could conduct small talk with no difficulty. Danny, my predecessor in the position, had been forced to leave Italy urgently for personal reasons, so I didn't receive the benefit of his experience. Still, in a relatively short time I got my bearings at work. The contact man I worked with was the military attaché in Rome, Colonel Ruben Ashkenazi from the navy (who succeeded Zvi Alon in the position). With Ruben and his wife Zipora we forged strong ties of friendship. In my new position I was in charge of supervising Mabat's business relations with various marine weapon factories in Italy. I also supervised the work of Israeli teams in four different locations, which involved traveling throughout the country.

During the first weeks I inquired as to who was responsible for technical writing in the weapon factories. I discovered that this duty was assigned to a man named Aldo Restani, who managed along with his brother a company for technical writing in La Spezia. Aldo turned out to be an exceptionally kind, clever and humane individual. We soon became friends. I learned that during World War II Aldo assisted Jews and helped illegal immigrants sail to Palestine. He even published essays in British newspapers condemning the immigration policy of the Mandate. Through Aldo I came to know the warmth and humanity of the Italian people. Through him I also became acquainted with Italian food. On the coast near La Spezia there is a place called *Cinque Terre* (Five Islands). It is a beautiful place, with excellent restaurants serving choice delicacies. Each time I visited him, Aldo invited me to dine with him in one of these restaurants. Among other things he taught me how to drink Fernet-Branca, a bittersweet liquor that aficionados drink at the end of the meal to help digest the food. I found the liquor much to my liking, adopting the habit enthusiastically, and even today finish my meal with a glass. During our stay in Italy I used to visit La Spezia with Chaya and the children. Every time we came Aldo would invite us to dine with him in the finest restaurants and treat us with the greatest warmth and congeniality. He gave the children all kinds of presents, so it was no wonder they warmed up to him, and we all felt that we had a tender and devoted friend in La Spezia.

In time Chaya and I learned to adapt to life in Italy under the assumption that "When in Rome, act like a Roman." We took that proverb quite literally. I learned to dress in an adorned, elegant manner, as befit my status as a representative of a respected company. I knew that Italians cared about quality apparel and the trends of fashion, so I bought expensive suits and fine silk ties. More than once, during a meeting, a colleague would ask to examine my tie, and he almost always knew the material and the fashion house where it was purchased. Chaya also adorned herself in beautiful, elegant clothes, since in Italy a woman's apparel is no less important than a man's. We would have preferred to refrain from spending excessive amounts of money on clothes, but my professional position forced us into the habit. And yet, although I had some money and an expense account at my disposal, we always tried to act modestly. I was careful to sleep in modest hotels, to eat in average restaurants and to drive a simple Fiat.

I became acquainted with the Italian folk and discovered them to be happy, people-loving, and teeming with human warmth. The humane attitude of the Italian people was evident even in the harsh days of World War II. Even though Fascism developed in Italy and Mussolini instituted the Race Laws as early as 1938, no Jews were physically harmed until the

Nazi invasion in 1943. As long as it was possible, the Italian people tried to protect the Jewish citizens of their country. The Jewish community in Italy was small but ancient, and its roots date back to before the destruction of the Second Temple. The members of the community adopted the Italian language and culture and, barring religious traditions and rituals, the Jews became well integrated among the country's inhabitants.

During my stay in Italy I found that most of the people I knew had warm, healthy social relationships, treating each other in a graceful, friendly manner. Nevertheless, here and there I found shortcomings in "the Italian mentality." These faults sometimes damaged our working relations. While in Italy I noticed that the Italians put a lot of emphasis on the pleasures of life and dedicated a considerable portion of their time to leisure activities and recreation. Many of the people I knew gave these pleasures such high priority, that they were often glad to "sacrifice" work and business on the altar of life's delights. As a result, at times, I came up against a frivolous attitude toward work. In my first days in Italy I was amazed by this flippant attitude and saw it as an obstacle to working relations. It seemed to me that my Italian colleagues were more intent on recreation and leisure time than on keeping regular working hours. One day, after I had made a remark to a factory director about a delay in shipments, he took the occasion to invite me to one of his factory's staff meetings to show me how he reprimands his employees. I arrived at the meeting, we drank a few cups of coffee and aperitifs, and each of the engineers and division managers gave a report on his activities, all the while making all sorts of excuses for his lack of progress. After they had all finished giving their accounts, the director festively opened a beautiful silver box. "Look, Mr. Shachar is here, and I'm beginning to get mad," he said cheerfully, "If I hear anymore stories and evasions, I will have to start taking valium pills from this box." He added while pointing at the box, "And you wouldn't want your director to start living on valium pills, right?"

I had expected him to fire at least one of his subordinates, and his conduct left me stunned. Eventually I understood that this was his management style and, having no other alternative, I got used to it. In the end, one way or another, the needed results were achieved.

Another difficulty I met in my contact with local colleagues also originated from the Italian mindset. Often my Italian colleagues would talk in a roundabout way, and only after trust was established would they come forward with their real intentions. As someone accustomed to the straightforward and purposeful discourse used in Israel, I sometimes found it difficult to provide an adequate account when reporting back to my superiors at home. Being ignorant of the local style, they demanded concrete data about my meetings and the development of the businesses I managed – data I often couldn't provide.

The prevailing opinion ascribes the Italians an excessive love for the arts, and a predilection toward preserving and protecting their national heritage. In my humble opinion, this predisposition does not stem from national and ideological motivations, but from a desire to preserve the hedonistic lifestyle, abounding with *joie de vivre*, manifesting in the Italians' love for food, wardrobe, women and sex. Thus, for example, I witnessed their extreme resentment toward the penetration of American influence into various areas of their life. When fast-food chains began sprouting up in Rome, the older restaurant owners took to the streets with pots of traditional dishes and tried to convince the Italian teenagers not to buy fast food. When the jeans fashion appeared, the Italian designer stood up for the local fashion industry. The admirers of Italian song battled the infiltration of pop and rock music. But eventually nothing could stop the American way of life from permeating Italy as well, as it did in so many other places throughout the world.

Enjoying life, I discovered among a few of my Italian friends, preceded even the accepted moral laws, and many of them unscrupulously violated the sanctity of marriage. One time an Italian friend of mine spoke to me of his extramarital relations and described them thus: "To my eyes, having extramarital relationships is actually altruism. I love women and I have lots of money. Every woman I'm having a relationship with receives kind treatment, clothes and presents from me. If I could benefit five women simultaneously, why should the laws of morality force me to benefit only one?"

In time Chaya and I made several Italian friends. In Rome we befriended Gustavo, one of the owners of a factory for delicate mechanical instruments which also produced military equipment. Gustavo was wealthy, kind and generous, and a true companion and conversationalist. A few times we stayed as guests in his house on a small island called

Gianutri, also known as *Isola Senza Tempo* (Island without Time), located three miles off the western coast of Italy. We used to arrive by yacht. We met and learned to like his wife Paula, a pleasant French woman.

In Florence we became good friends with two couples. The first couple was Bruno Natale, who was a member of the board in a factory we did business with, and his Spanish wife Teresa, of whom we were especially fond. The other couple, Alberto Fiorinti and his wife, lived in an interesting villa on one of Florence's hills. He was the owner of a shipping company whose services we used from time to time. On several occasions we got to visit his awe-inspiring home. The house, built in the twelfth century, had once been a convent, and gardens and citrus trees grew all around it. Close to the main residence was another room which was the convent's *batistero* – the baptizing room. Its impressive walls were decorated with drawings, and Alberto had transformed it into an enchanting music room.

We also befriended a Venetian Jew named Umberto Navarro and his wife Gabriella. We were introduced to them by Anna, the owner of the apartment in Via Flaminia. Anna was also the owner of the Anna Moda Fashion House, an elite sewing workshop where Rome's high society women, as well as famous actresses, had their clothes made. Anna rented the workshop from Umberto.

The Navarros, well-known sympathizers of Israel, were warm, effervescent people, but they had not been blessed with children. They resided on the hills of Tuscany in a grand villa. In the yard, on a pole, a flag of Israel danced in the wind. Umberto explained that he reached an agreement with the local police people by which the plot he lives on was considered Israeli territory. As long as the bribes arrived on time, the Italian authorities had no qualms with the foreign flag. Toward Passover Umberto used to prepare kosher Passover wine in his "Israeli Territory."

Umberto and Gabriella would invite us every once in a while to a festive lunch in their villa on a Saturday afternoon. At these meals there were usually some interesting Italian girls who contributed to the vibrant, vivacious atmosphere. To these very same meals Umberto would invite from time to time one of Italy's leading rabbis. The rabbi, a strict man of religion, used to bring his own kosher plates and cutlery, since he was meticulous about such matters. The revelry and the women, however, didn't seem to bother him at all. He mingled well with the happy company. The respected rabbi, who didn't resemble at all the rabbi figure I remembered from my childhood in Poland, was also a worldly scholar and held a PhD in theology and philosophy. He showed a deep understanding and knowledge of art. A number of times he accompanied Chaya and me on a visit to the adjacent town, Faienza, where spectacular Renaissance paintings were on display. There he would provide us with fascinating, educated explanations on the value of the Christian paintings.

A few years later, when Umberto and Gabriella visited Israel, I wanted to return some of the abundance they had imparted to us. To that end I asked my friend, Ben-Eliezer, to bring them to meet his friend, a major in active duty, who then invited them for a visit to one of the IDF's outposts. Gabriella brought with her, as a gift for the soldiers, sacks full of pasta, olive oil and parsley. She then proceeded to cook them an Italian delicacy. Their host, the major, said that he had never seen such a party. Gabriella looked very happy too. She felt grateful for the chance she got to cook one of her culinary delights for the soldiers of the IDF.

In the summer of 1973, after serving two successful years as a representative of Mabat in Italy, I was appointed representative of the entire IAI in Italy. In conjunction with my new appointment I was charged with the supervision of advanced defense equipment manufacture in the entire area, including Switzerland. At the same time I was asked to continue representing Mabat's interests. In those days the aircraft industry was responsible for a slew of technological systems in the entire IDF, not just in the air force. Consequently, the promotion was a significant one – from representing a factory of two thousand workers to one representing an industry employing twenty-four thousand men and women. In those days I retained one secretary, but I worked with heads of staff in many factories. I was also put in charge of additional factories in cities throughout Italy. I began to function in different fields as well – financial, contractual, technological – in addition to those of politics and intelligence.

Despite the great satisfaction I got from my work, I was forced to deal with pressure from different sources. The heads of different companies in the IAI working in Israel wanted me to purchase certain products for them and market others, and now and again complained that I didn't execute their business for them to their complete satisfaction. It is quite possible that a bit of jealousy crept into their complaints – jealousy of the successes I had and the giant scope of the deals I conducted. In spite of all this, I was later appreciated and admired for my achievements.

During the Yom Kippur War we lost contact with our son Zohar for a while. We received word that he had been called up and was serving as a shell loader in a tank in the Golan Heights. Apart from that we knew nothing, and our worries gave us no rest. I used my contacts with the Military Attaché and the IAI to update myself on his condition. In this way we found out that Syrian commandos had taken control of armored forces in the area my son fought in, taking the soldiers as prisoners.

We were frantic with worry. Finally news of our eldest son arrived. Fortunately and to our great joy, Zohar survived the war unharmed and upon its conclusion returned to complete his studies at the Technion.

Later we found out that Dudu Yishai, the son of my friend Elhanan Yishai, was killed in a battle in the Suez Canal. Only a short while before the war, after completing his regular army service, Dudu toured Europe, and for a few weeks we had the pleasure of accommodating him at our home in Italy. We toured Italy with him and had a delightful time together, and at his request I arranged a job for him in a workshop for the repair and maintenance of ski equipment. When the Yom Kippur War broke out he decided of his own free will to go home and enlist. In the second day of the war he disappeared, and only six months later his body was recovered from a tank in the Suez Canal area. His parents were heartbroken by their loss. They published a memorial booklet in his memory, entitled *At Breaking Point*.

The war created great pressure at work, even after the fighting was over, since much of the IDF's equipment had been exhausted. I and the other representatives were charged with the task of purchasing and obtaining the weaponry, spare parts and ammunition to send to Israel. To this end we contacted defense industries all over Italy, as well as different branches of the Italian military.

When the war was over the IDF sent high-ranking officers to Italy to make purchasing contracts and get updated in different fields. This also afforded the officers a much-needed break after the grueling months of war. We were happy to entertain some of these officers, including the heads of the air force and the navy.

One day I was asked to host a high-ranking officer who had distinguished himself in the "Chinese Farm" battle near the Suez Canal. I decided to invite him and his family to one of the most prestigious restaurants in Italy.

While the waiter lengthily explained the wine list, their quality and vintage, I noticed the distinguished officer reading the list as if he were reading a dull catalog. As soon as the waiter finished his explanations the children asked for Coca-Cola. I ordered one of the wines myself, but my guests didn't indulge in a single sip. Afterwards the waiter described the various delicacies available on the menu, but the kids insisted upon schnitzel and French fries. I translated the request to the waiter. "Please," he said contemptuously, "there is none of that kind of garbage in our restaurant." The man finally agreed to send one of his junior waiters to a cheap restaurant nearby, and from there he brought us the schnitzel and fries. We paid handsomely for this service, ten times what we would have paid had we actually eaten in the nearby restaurant.

Of all the matters I dealt with during my time in Italy, one in particular took the most time and effort. In 1973 the IAI decided to purchase thirteen second-hand Boeing planes from an American company, renovate them at the shops of the corporation and later sell them at a profit. But when news of the decision was published in Israel, it immediately caused a wave of criticism. It was inconceivable, the critics argued, that government companies would make a deal with private companies without the approval of the government. The corporation then decided to drop the whole business. In other words, to sell all the planes as soon as possible. In a telegram I received from Al Schwimmer, the CEO of the IAI, he said that "every delegate abroad must make the utmost effort to sell the Boeing 707s."

Through Amos Ginor, the aircraft marketing manager, we got in contact with a number of Italian pilots who had decided at that time to establish a private airline company called Europa. The pilots showed an interest in our offer and were willing to purchase a few of the Boeings. The head of the company was a pilot named Mario Berchini, a son of a military physician of noble birth who fought in World War II for the Axis and participated in the attack on the USSR. We wrote up a contract with the Italian company, and in it was stated that payment would be spread out in a few monthly payments. Simultaneously we arranged financial guarantees from a bank in England, but unfortunately, difficulties arose in the closing of the deal. Alitalia Airlines, which until then had a monopoly on the airline business in Italy, made it difficult to get authorization for the activation of a new airline. In order to get the permit we had to use contacts in parliament, and to that end Berchini approached Doctor Mario Liguori, a general in the reserves with a PhD in economics. (The Italians give the title of doctor to any university graduate. I was called "*Doctor Enginira*," and I was asked to sign official papers using that title, since it was unreasonable that a respected company would appoint a man without a title to this kind of high-ranking position.)

Doctor Liguori had some contacts in the Christian-Democratic party which was in control of Italy at the time. In addition he was the head of the Pantheon Club, which conducted the party's business outside of parliament, and its members were ministers and powerful industrialists. Liguori informed me that he had scheduled a meeting with the party CEO in parliament in order to advance the matter of authorization for the young company. Despite my fears of being associated with a political party while I was working at the embassy, I had to prepare myself for the important meeting. I purchased a camel-hair coat, whose price was higher than my monthly salary, and an expensive fur hat. Thus elegantly attired, I reported to the meeting in the parliament building in Rome at the side of Doctor Liguori. Guards in colorful uniforms, wearing feathered hats and armed with spears, announced our arrival, and led us through the parliament hallways. I felt like I was taking part in some bizarre ritual, until finally we arrived at the office of the party CEO.

We were invited into a luxuriously furnished office, richly decorated with mementos, antiques and other pieces of art. Doctor Liguori introduced me as "the head of the Israel Aircraft Industries," and asked the CEO for his authorization of an airline activation permit. He emphasized two main points. Firstly, the airline would supply jobs for unemployed Italian pilots. This justification particularly touched the Italians' hearts, especially the southern politicians, who were known for their huge sensitivity toward social matters. The State of Israel, Doctor Ligueri promised, would assist in resources, tools, instruction and financial credit. Furthermore, stressed the honorable doctor, it would help the fledgling State of Israel, many of whose citizens are victims of the Holocaust who were fighting for its survival. The CEO was inclined to agree with the points made by the honorable doctor, and he took notes.

He promised he would try to act on the matter, and nothing remained for me to do but to show him my sincerest gratitude. It should be mentioned that in addition to the fundamental considerations we had mentioned, which should have encouraged him to act, Europa Airlines transfered a large sum to his party's account. In only a few days the CEO succeeded in gaining parliament approval for our request allowing Europa Airlines to fly in Italian skies, though it would still be subject to a number of strict rules. We were very thankful for the decision, and one of the two Boeings was immediately flown to Italy. The new airline began operating. It mainly ran flights to holiday resorts in North Africa and Spain (one time I had the honor of flying with them as a paying passenger to England). The money flowed into the company's account, and from there to the IAI. I was charged with payment supervision. At some point the company people decided to sell it to a rich Italian businessman, and he continued to operate it and close its debts.

I was also responsible for the well-being of the Israeli maintenance team sent over to accompany the plane. The team numbered eight technicians. One of them, A, had previously been a member of the IAI's employee committee. He was sent to Italy, because he often criticized members of the management. They decided to send him out of the country for a time and Italy was chosen as a suitable destination. Upon arrival in Rome, A began demanding special, unconventional perks for himself, under threat that if I should not accommodate him he would lodge a complaint against me or sabotage my relations with the various factory representatives in Italy. I was advised by many to consent to his demands to prevent retribution. I realized that I was dealing with a problematic person and endeavored to fulfill his requests. However, in reports I sent to Israel I wrote that he was a disturbing and disruptive factor. Regretfully, copies of these reports fell into his hands, and our relationship became very tense.

In mid-1974, serious problems began appearing in the Europa Airlines company. Its owner ventured to open new air routes for the company, but Alitalia Airlines vetoed the idea. Internal disputes and conflicts broke out among the company's pilots, and these quickly began affecting the management of the business. Two months later the company directors discontinued the payments for one of the planes they had purchased from us. From Israel I was pressured to extricate the plane and return it home before the London bank confiscated it. One Sunday, at four in the morning, I approached the small Champino airport near Rome along with an Israeli pilot and the plane's maintenance team. Two crates of whisky was all it took for the forward air controller to approve takeoff.

A beneficial result of the whole Boeing affair was the excellent relationships I formed with a number of people. My relations with Doctor Liguori benefited me significantly in my future business dealings. He introduced me to people from the high echelons of society, both in government and business, in Italy and the Vatican. Doctor Liguori presented me as an expert on the most modern and advanced technologies. I utilized these contacts for the IAI's benefit, and signed many good deals on its behalf. A few of these deals were eventually annulled, since the Ministry of Defense didn't approve the commissions Doctor Liguori requested for himself. At times Doctor Liguori, who saw me as a representative of the Jewish world, introduced me to various personages in the Vatican, with whom I debated and discussed matters of faith. For me these sessions were especially engaging and challenging.

As a result of the Boeing incident I also deepened my relationship with the pilot Mario Berchini. He would invite me and my guests to enjoy the bohemian districts of Rome with him, especially L'arciliuto, a club featuring Neapolitan singing in the former studio of the famous painter Raphael. Berchini would later come to Israel as a representative of various companies, and to this day we still keep in touch.

Another area that demanded significant effort on my part was the issue of "Repeated Purchase." According to the Knesset's legislation, for every Israeli purchase of a foreign product, the product's seller must be persuaded to spend at least 20 percent of the product's value on exported Israeli products. This would insure that foreign currency would flow back into the country. My part in this lay in convincing a variety of factories to buy Israeli products, especially of IAI manufacture. Often the products wouldn't suit the clients and their standards, or they were more expensive than similar European products. On other occasions the prospective clients could manufacture the products themselves. Despite these hindrances I occasionally succeeded in convincing the Italians to purchase IAI products for millions of dollars – an achievement that the IAI considered most impressive.

The law concerning repeated purchase allowed representatives of Israeli manufacturers to come to Italy and help conduct the sales. These visits didn't always prove useful, but the representatives enjoyed touring Italy. We played host for them – we traveled the length and breadth of Italy with them, dined them in restaurants, invited them to concerts and took them shopping. As enjoyable as this sounds, it demanded a significant time investment, and sometimes we would sink under the weight of the task.

Still, Italy was good for me. In addition to the great satisfaction I received from work, I was exposed to a new and different world of indulgence and self-gratification. Inch by inch I learned from the Italians how to enjoy my free time through leisure and family activities. Often, I would take Chaya and the kids on vacations and trips, especially on weekends and national holidays. We toured various regions of Italy, including Florence, Torino, Milan and Venice. Eventually we expanded the scope of our travels – to Aix-les-Bains and Grenoble in France, where I introduced the family to the various places where I had grown up. We also toured Greece, Sicily, Spain, Switzerland, England and the Scandinavian lands. We even went as far as the United States and visited my relatives there.

In the summer months we loved to drive to the beach on the Italian or French Riviera. In the winter we visited ski resorts. I was familiar with skiing from my childhood days in Russia. There I used to make my way to school on skis like all the other kids. However, only in Italy did I learn to really love skiing. I stayed at famous ski lodges across Europe, especially the Grand Sasso (Great Rock) in the Abruzzo district in the Apennine Mountains. The peaks in that area tower as high as three thousand meters, with picturesque villages peppered at their feet, whose entire communities live off the skiing industry.

Our Italy adventure stretched to five years. In that time I had, of course, kept in constant telephone contact with my mother. She didn't like the decision we had made to work in Italy, which in her eyes represented the cradle of Christianity, and she didn't approve of our prolonging our stay, but as was always her way she respected our wishes and refrained from criticizing our decision.

Because I had fulfilled my duty in the best possible way, my superiors offered to prolong my stay for another period. But by this time Noam had come of age for conscription and most of all we missed our eldest son Zohar more than ever. Furthermore, problems had arisen regarding the apartment we had rented in Israel. Despite the offer made to me by the IAI's Board of Directors, we decided to leave Italy in 1976 and return to Israel.

The years we lived in Italy benefited my family and especially myself. I succeeded in my work, took advantage of the possibilities Italy opened up for me, and no less important – I was enriched by the many social relations I had established with Italian colleagues. To this day I take pleasure in speaking with my friends on the telephone, and I need only a few moments of conversation to relive the wondrous life I had there. During my visits to Italy I visit friends and enjoy every moment.

CHAPTER TEN

Resuming Work at the Israel Aircraft Industries

In the summer of 1976, after an absence of five years, the four of us – Chaya, Noam, Lior and I – returned to Israel.

While we were in Italy we had put our apartment in Israel up for rent. However, no tenants could be found for it in the final year of our stay in Italy and it remained empty for all that time. The friend to whom we had entrusted the keys had left the windows open and the apartment had become infested with birds and their nests. The furniture was completely destroyed. After we got over the initial shock, we cleaned the apartment thoroughly, replaced the furniture with new items we had brought with us from Italy, and returned to live in it.

While we were still in Italy our son Zohar announced that he intended to marry his sweetheart, a girl named Ella who was studying education at Haifa University. Zohar had met Ella during his studies in the Technion. We advised him to wait a little, since he was only twenty-one, but the young couple insisted. Following our return to Israel in September 1976, the two got married. Two years later, in 1978, their daughter Maya was born, our first granddaughter. The years went by, and these days our Maya is completing her bachelor's degree in humanities and social studies.

Noam enlisted in the army. His teachers in Italy were impressed by his academic accomplishments and recommended that he pursue higher education in mathematics. They even offered to send a recommendation letter to the military authorities requesting to postpone his recruitment. But he refused their offer and insisted on enlisting. He wanted to join the army with all his friends from Israel. He was accepted and enrolled in the air force's pilots course, where he acquitted himself successfully. But in one of the final stages of the course he reached the conclusion that he wasn't inclined toward flying and he decided to dismiss himself. He was transferred to the artillery corps, where he excelled as an officer and a battery commander.

Lior returned to the Korczak school in Ramat Gan. The five-year absence had caused him to forget some of his Hebrew. Since his Hebrew was weak and he was also one of the youngest in his grade, Chaya suggested that he remain behind one grade. The principal consented to her recommendation and Lior integrated quickly and seemed content with the decision.

And as for me – at that stage of my life I could have chosen an independent business career and made use of the many professional contacts I had made in Italy. However, because of ethical concerns I restrained myself from using contacts from my public position to further my personal interests – at least for a reasonable "cooling off" period. And thus, after a short unpaid vacation, I resumed working at the IAI. The decision to return to the same organization was not at all easy. I was disappointed that the IAI managers failed to fulfill their promise to appoint me as the Israeli contact for Europa Airlines. Instead, I was given the position of Coordinator of Israel Aircraft Delegations Abroad. I found the position boring, since most delegations were not interested in anyone meddling in their affairs and coordinating between them. Therefore, in my free time and under my own initiative I helped Europe Desk director Haim Kenet as much as I could, especially in initiating business deals in Italy and France. I couldn't help but feel the reservations of some managers in the IAI who felt that I had not acted in their favor during my time in Italy.

After a while, the late Aryeh Ostrinsky, assistant director of the IAI, offered me the directorship of one of IAI's factories. The factory was located in Bnei Yehuda, a communal settlement in the south of the Golan Heights.

It manufactured ejector seats. "Look," I answered him, "After seven years of living in Kiryat Shmona, my wife and children don't want to relocate north again, especially to the Golan Heights which is so far from the center." My refusal wasn't accepted gracefully. Members of the board thought I wanted to avoid my duties or that I tended toward exaggerated self-importance.

In 1977 I decided to realize my unfulfilled intellectual ambitions. I signed up for studies in the Faculty for Political Science and Economy in Bar Ilan University, and I attended courses on Judaism, psychology, and sociology. I derived great pleasure from my classes. Although I had chosen a career in the technological sciences, I had always been attracted to the social sciences and humanities. I integrated my work with my studies and often I would feel the weight of these opposite commitments. More than once I had to forego lectures in favor of one of my superior's requests. My frequent trips abroad on matters of business disrupted my studies further. Nevertheless, in 1982 I completed my bachelor's degree. I had succeeded.

I wasn't the first or only student in the family. Chaya preempted me. In 1976 she signed up for education, Bible and art studies in the Tel Aviv branch of the Hebrew University of Jerusalem. As expected, she enjoyed great satisfaction from her studies. Our second trip to Italy, on which I will expand presently, cut off her studies just as she was about to complete her degree, but she finished it immediately upon her return to Israel.

In the meantime Noam finished three years of regular service and two years of career service in the IDF. In 1980 he was discharged, and he began studying mathematics and physics at the Hebrew University of Jerusalem. There he met a young student named Iris. The two studied together for one year, after which they decided to quit university and get married. Noam commenced work in Classica, a company that imported products for diplomats.

Our son Lior studied in the Blich High School in Ramat Hen.

Throughout this entire period I kept in close contact with my mother and brother. My mother lived in Kiryat Ata with one of my brother's daughters, and she still subsisted on the modest income she received as compensation from Germany. On Purim – one of the only holidays in which it is permitted to travel according to Jewish law – all of the brothers living in Israel and their offspring would get together in my brother Aharon's house.

I have never ceased having the utmost appreciation and admiration for my mother. I admire her strength of spirit, her faith and her openness. Even though she was an Orthodox woman and kept all the commandments, she always took a practical approach toward problems – as long as it wasn't an affront to God's name. Often she would quote the phrase, "A stupid Jew is worse than a converted Jew." Moreover, she always kept herself involved and influenced her surroundings. One day a tragedy fell on her neighbors, Holocaust survivors and God-fearing people like herself. Their beloved daughter was killed in a tractor accident. The mother fell into deep despair, set her daughter's picture on the table, lit candles around it and continued to grieve for many days. One day the woman's husband approached my mother and shared his twofold pain with her – sorrow for his daughter lost in the accident and for his wife lost to grief. Upon hearing the husband's words, my mother entered their house, walked up to the daughter's photograph, shattered it to pieces, and snuffed out the candles. The startled woman began to protest. "By the laws of highest providence, the Jewish people are allowed seven days of mourning and thirty more days of lamentation until the visit to the grave." My mother admonished her resolutely. "After that, our masters taught, we go on living. Now, get up from your chair of grief, go to the bathroom, clean yourself up and come back to life. I won't leave you be until you do so." And thus it was.

My mother also kept an eye on the relationships of her sons and their wives. She would often side with her daughters-in-law, and she used to remind me and my brothers to buy our wives flowers on their birthdays, since she knew we tended to forget.

In her last years she suffered from internal bleeding, and once in a while she lost enough blood to need infusions. Nevertheless, she kept her lucidity and faith, kept on reading the Book of Psalms and Tzena Urena (a book of homilies for Jewish women from the sixteenth century), and she was aware and alert almost to her very last day. In 1981 her situation deteriorated and she was hospitalized in the Rambam hospital until her subsequent death. My mother encountered incredible hardships throughout her life, but she lived to see grandchildren and great-grandchildren of which she was very proud. My brother Yosef passed away three years later, due to heart problems and asthma, leaving behind a loving family.

CHAPTER ELEVEN

We Return to Italy – Representing Tahal

One day I met Aryeh Gisin, a friend of mine from the distant Kiryat Shmona days. Aryeh informed me that he was the director of Tahal (Water Planning for Israel). After we had updated each other on our respective situations, Aryeh asked for my help on a certain project in Italy. At the time, Tahal was serving as a subcontractor in a project called the Biafra Restoration Plan. According to the plan, the Italian government gave assistance to different African nations, which in turn were required to purchase Italian projects with Italian workforces, services and gear. As part of this plan Italy was assisting Nigeria in restoring Biafra's economy after the great famine that had crippled it in the '80s. The Italians made use of several Israeli companies (Tahal among them) for the task of gathering information in Biafra. There was need of intelligence in such areas as transportation, economy, education and agriculture. As a result of a recommendation I made, Tahal decided to hire the services of an old friend of mine, an electrical engineer named Roberto. I met Roberto during my work in Italy.

Eventually it became clear that the match between Roberto and Tahal was not working as well as we'd hoped, and Aryeh suggested that I fly to Italy to try and fill Roberto's position. He was in effect offering me a job. As part of an attempt to establish an Italian company that would be responsible for managing the project in Biafra, I would be working opposite the Nigerians on the one hand, opposite the large Italian contractor that had undertaken the management of the program on the other and alongside the Israeli subcontractors on the third. My task was to divide the funds among the various bodies in the most optimal manner. I was delighted to hear Aryeh's offer. It had been six years since I had returned from Italy and the beautiful memories lingering in my mind urged me to agree to his offer and return. Unfortunately, as a result of the urgency of Tahal's offer I could not negotiate the terms of my retirement from IAI in the best possible way, and eventually retired with less auspicious benefits than I had hoped for.

In June 1982, Chaya, Lior and I boarded a flight to Italy. For the first few months we rented a furnished, air-conditioned apartment in a lodging house in the Friuli district in northern Rome. The building provided various services, including room cleaning. The living quarters were very comfortable, though the rent was understandably rather high.

We enrolled Lior in a prodigious English secondary school in Rome. He put a lot of effort into the subjects he loved, especially art and history. But after finishing twelfth grade in 1983, he purchased a plane ticket for himself and returned to Israel. He said that in order to "build himself" he had to work in physical labor, and in the time he had left before enlisting in the IDF he worked at different jobs: moving, fishing and a personal delivery business which he ran with a partner. In 1984 Lior enlisted in the IDF and served on a missile boat in the navy.

Chaya and I were left alone in Rome, but we felt neither lonely nor miserable. We moved to an apartment next to my office in Guido d'Arezzo Street. Chaya recommenced her regular meetings with girlfriends from our previous time in Rome. She regularly visited museums and galleries under the guide of an art teacher, and enjoyed those days very much.

As part as my new work, I founded Planital, the Italian company responsible for implementing the Biafra Restoration Plan in Nigeria. Eight workers were employed in the company. Four people gathered field data in Nigeria, and four more worked in the office in Rome, mainly processing data and planning the project. I was in charge of managing the workers, distributing the money and overseeing relations with the Italians. In areas pertaining to engineering, economy, agriculture and so forth, I was aided by professionals from Tahal.

I was greatly satisfied with my job, but also burdened with heavy responsibility. Again I had to entertain many guests – Israeli, Italian and Nigerian. The Nigerians always came wearing their traditional garb – colorful capes and hats and loud necklaces that drew attention everywhere. One day I invited a chief to a fish restaurant and instructed the waiter to offer him the best entrées in the menu. My guest chose a certain fish and the waiter filleted it, expertly removing the skeleton and seasoning it with wine and lemon before serving it to my guest. But the chief desired only the heads of the fish we had ordered. The waiter explained that he had disposed of the heads, whereupon I proposed that the waiter prepare two more fish, of which he would bring only the heads, and then the fish themselves could be sold to other customers. So the waiter served the guest four fish heads. The chief sucked the heads a long while, and I paid a hefty bill.

Most of the Israeli guests weren't accommodated in our apartment but in a hotel. Nevertheless they expected me to devote many hours of my time to them and keep them entertained during their stay. This required much effort on my part. Chaya often had to accompany the wives of the envoys on tours, shopping trips and museum visits. More than once we were embarrassed by our guests' behavior. One day Chaya was touring the Vatican with her guest, a woman who was very respected in Israel. Suddenly the woman burst out at their tour guide – "all these ornaments were stolen from the Temple!" Another time, I was walking with one of our female guests in Rome, and after I had shown her the beautiful red bricks in the ancient part of the city she said, "Say, why are all the bricks here red? Wouldn't it be better to splash some white on them? Why don't you import some white paint to Rome?"

Many of my guests didn't know how to enjoy the food the Italian kitchen had to offer. For example, when we came to Italian restaurants, after the guests were offered an abundance of pastas, they actually frowned at the fact that they couldn't have Pasta Osem, the Israeli brand. The numerous dinners I organized, especially the duties of sharing alcoholic drinks with my guests, were quite abusive to my health.

Nevertheless we didn't suffer – the opposite is true. It was a period saturated with delights. We were both alone, and could therefore make the most out of our free time. Almost every weekend and on vacations we went on trips outside of Rome, to places like Palma de Mallorca, Switzerland and Sicily. On one occasion Lior came for a visit, and we went with him to Sicily. On the road there, near the city of Catania, we were caught in a large traffic jam. I was driving, Lior was sleeping in the back seat and Chaya was sitting next to me with her purse placed next to her. As we were slowly inching forward, we noticed two people on motorcycles riding suspiciously close to our car. Suddenly one of them opened the car door and started pulling Chaya's purse. I pulled the purse's strap from my side and tried to resist him, while still driving slowly forward and keeping my hand on the horn to alert others of our situation. My efforts were unsuccessful, and the purse was stolen. This caused us some distress, since the purse held a large amount of cash, the keys to our apartment, and extra keys to the car. Out of fear that the thieves would break into our house or steal our car, we decided to terminate our vacation, return home to Rome and change all the locks. In retrospect we discovered that the robbers targeted us because our car sported Roman license plates. The Sicilians, we discovered, do not approve of the elitist citizens of the capital.

In 1983 I signed up for a master's degree in Business Administration in the Roman branch of the University of Washington. I greatly enjoyed my studies and was even a prominent student, but the management of my company didn't view my studies favorably. They pressured me to discontinue my studies, claiming that it might disrupt my work. Eventually the verdict fell from on high, as that branch of the University of Washington had financial difficulties and was shut down.

During all the time I was active in Italy, negotiations continued with Roberto in spite of the great dissatisfaction prevalent on both sides. Since I was the initiator of this relationship I often received criticism and admonishment. He was said to be greedy and unprofessional. Eventually, I was ordered explicitly by Tahal's legal department to terminate relations with him. This put me in a difficult position. Roberto had built most of the systems operating in our project, systems considered to be of sensitive legal stature in Italy. Furthermore, many of the people attached to the project were his people, and I knew it would be tricky to untie all the connections he'd made and build new ones instead. I made one of the most difficult decisions of my professional life. I met with Roberto and explained to him that I would like to continue working with him without my superiors knowing about it, under the assumption that they wouldn't care who exactly runs the system as long as it is run well. At first, to test its liability, I didn't expose my decision to the management. But after awhile I decided to tell them that I was still working with the mechanism set up by Roberto. "If you fail this time as well," they warned, "it's all over for you." To my great relief I managed to patch things up with Roberto and things went mostly according to plan.

Despite this, tensions and anxiety were building up. Some of the office holders in the company didn't approve of the success and advancement of an outsider, as well as the independent initiatives that I carried out.

Meanwhile, Aryeh Gisin quit his position as director of Tahal, and Yossi Maayan (later CEO of the Ministry of Defense) was appointed in his stead. When Gisin departed I was left without an advocate from within Tahal.

After two and a half years, instead of the three we had agreed upon, the decision was made to terminate relations with me. Nevertheless, I was promised the full compensation stated in the contract. I received the decision willingly, since I was ripe to leave my position anyway.

In September 1984 I finished my job with Tahal, but I felt the need to straighten things out so as to leave in a dignified manner. I asked for an arbitrator to judge between us. Aryeh Gisin took the task upon himself and ruled that Tahal had not shown me fair treatment. He emphasized the fact that in spite of differences of opinion, I had fulfilled all my obligations thoroughly and had executed all the tasks put upon me with minimum expense.

In the few months I was in Italy after my resignation from Tahal I managed to found another company with an old Italian friend of mine by the name of Georgio de la Roca, an Italian Jew who was an accountant by trade. Georgio and I established Isital, a company for the distribution of Israeli electronic devices in Italy. We employed a technician and opened an office and lab in Campo de Fiori, one of Rome's more picturesque squares, alongside flower, fruit and vegetable markets. Chaya and I moved to an apartment building not far from there. We later opened another office next to Piazza Navona (in a building belonging to the Federici family, a famous pasta manufacturer). As our first project we marketed a device for fingerprint identification invented by an Israeli company which was the first of its kind in the country. We believed that the banks would gladly incorporate the device in their ATM system, and that they could use it to allow access to classified areas. We called the banks and offered them the device. They showed great interest, but it soon became clear that the device was not efficient enough and the company that had invented it went out of business. We lost a large amount of money as well – especially Georgio, who had invested most of his fortune and had dreamed of success. In spite of failure and the disintegration of the dream to become rich, Georgio and I remained good friends. Under the circumstances, this was nothing short of remarkable.

In March of 1985 Chaya and I returned to Israel. We were glad to be close to our children again, especially Lior who was serving in the military at the time. We resumed living in our apartment in Ramat Gan, which had been vacated in the meantime. Chaya began working as a teacher's instructor in the Yachad project – a tutoring program initiated by the Education Bureau and the Hebrew University of Jerusalem in which upperclassmen tutored underclassmen. I engaged in various business ventures, until in 1988 I decided to shift my attention to communal objectives.

CHAPTER TWELVE

Commemorating the Past

For many years after the conclusion of World War II I had wanted to carry out two important missions. One – to find my father's burial place, so I could say Kaddish at his grave. The other – to erect a monument in memory of the Jews who served in Poland's exiled armies during World War II, and fell in the battles against the Nazis. After the end of the Communist regime in Eastern Europe in 1988, I knew the time was ripe to make these goals a reality.

Ever since that fatal day when I saw my father for the last time, and even more after I heard Moshe Albrish's terrible account of the mass murder, I was never free of the desire to discover the fate of my father. I knew that I could never rest until I had thoroughly cleared up all the facts.

In 1965 I came upon a book entitled *The Rise and Fall of the Third Reich* by William L. Shirer. In one of its chapters, entitled "The First Days of Terror in Poland," I was astonished to read a description of the murder of about fifty Jews at the hands of Germans in Rozan (near Krasnosielc). The details of the incident accurately matched Moshe Albrish's testimony, and one paragraph in particular caught my attention – it stated that the soldiers who participated in the murders were court-martialed under Hitler's regime. During the trial the prosecutor demanded capital punishment for the defendants. They were eventually sentenced to life in prison, but the punished were later pardoned. The chapter also mentioned that news of the slaughter leaked to the newspapers and was exposed to the German public.

I later discovered that this had been the only time during the Nazi regime when SS soldiers were put on trail for the mass slaughter of Jews. In contrast, many soldiers were later put on trial for violations of discipline. A short time after the trial, on September 7, 1939, it was decided in the high echelons of the Third Reich that no more SS soldiers would stand trial for the murder of Jews. Such a procedure, they decided, went against the principles of the Reich. The decision was publicized in a formal edict published by Himmler on October 7, 1939. The edict said that SS soldiers would no longer be tried in the courts of the German military. They would instead stand trial in special tribunals – courts established especially for the SS units and manned by SS personnel. This cleared the way, naturally, for the murderers to commit atrocities without having to be punished. The publicized mass murder in Krasnosielc was apparently the first of its kind, the first mass slaughter of Jews by SS soldiers in Poland. The exposure of the incident in the media and the publication of the court's decision constitutes what is today an important historical reference point in studies of the Holocaust. Other facts mentioned in the book amazed me as well, which spurred me to continue investigating the details of this incident, all the while hoping that one day I would find my father's burial place.

After the fall of Communism, when Eastern European countries opened their doors to Western visitors, Chaya and I joined an organized group traveling to Poland, affording me the opportunity of visiting the country for the first time since I had left it. One day during the trip, Chaya and I abandoned our group, hired a local guide and took a cab to the town of Krasnosielc. I had been only nine years old when I had left the place, but the town had never left me. Childhood memories flooded me and I was overcome with emotion. I was astonished to find that almost nothing had changed. Most of the houses remained the way they were, except that all their Jewish residents were exchanged for Poles. I recognized familiar and beloved places where I had hung out with my childhood friends. I remembered their houses from days gone by. Our own house, however, was no longer – I later found out that it had been completely burned down in a fire shortly after the war ended. I wandered the streets of the town but didn't come across anybody familiar. Escorted by Chaya, I went to the place where I had bade my father goodbye. I stood in my place for a few minutes there, racked by an emotional storm. Later we walked to the town's synagogue. The building was still standing, but was now converted into a warehouse for agricultural products. Its new owner prevented me from entering.

I knew that the Polish I spoke might give me away and arouse the suspicion of the locals. I therefore asked our guide to help us. He asked the people of the town if they knew anything about Jews that had lived there and their slaughter. Their refusal to answer did not surprise us at all. They evaded our questions or simply declined to answer. Some of them even made such comments as "good riddance" when asked about the Jews. Even the mayor, a young person by the name of Miroslav Galinka, refused to volunteer information or even allow me to view the local archive where the history of the residents was documented. The visit ended without any substantial results.

In 1991 I traveled to Poland again and visited Krasnosielc. In that same trip I made a detour to the Jewish Historical Institute in Warsaw, where the chronicles of Poland's Jews are documented. I found only one document there pertaining to the Jews of Krasnosielc. The document, which was printed by the Poles and the Soviets in 1945, included among other things the testimony of a man named Richter, whom the Germans appointed mayor of the town during the war. He testified in the district court of Lomza concerning the slaughter that had occurred in the town. The document did not mention where the bodies were buried.

In 1993 I approached the military attaché of the German embassy in Tel Aviv, and asked him to assist me in locating the file of the trial in Germany's government archives. He agreed to my request, and contacted archival organizations in Germany, asking them to send him material on the subject. And indeed, that same year I received various documents connected with the trial. Among these I found two especially important papers which established beyond a shadow of a doubt the details of the incident and its consequences, exactly as they were described to me so many years ago. The first document, a report that was mailed from the Third Army to the Central Command of the Land Forces, detailed a court-martial of two soldiers serving in General Kampf's armored division for shooting fifty

Jews without provocation. The Jews had been repairing the bridge during the day. The report said that the prosecutor defined the soldiers' actions as murder and demanded a death sentence for them. One of the soldiers claimed there were mitigating circumstances. In his defense he said that the atrocities the Poles had done to the people of his country, native Germans, as well as the hostility of the Jews toward the Germans, had brought him to a state of high mental anxiety. He further pleaded in his defense that he acted out of youthful enthusiasm and without thought, and that he was a brave soldier who had never been punished before. At the trial's conclusion one defendant was sentenced to nine years in prison, while the other was only sentenced to three. Other documents showed that a few days after the report arrived, the commander of the Third Army decided to soften the punishment of the two soldiers – from nine years to a mere three years, from three years to a total revocation of the penalty.

The second document, no less important, was a copy of the Nurenberg Trial case file no. 12. The no. 12 trial took place between the years 1946 and 1948, and the defendant was Georg Von Küchler, commander of the Third Army. During this trial, General Kampf, who commanded the armored division deployed in the area at the time, testified that his troops attacked the Jews because they saw them as a threat. He emphasized the fact that he personally disapproved of this attitude. He continued to explain that the murder was committed by four SS men and another soldier belonging to the artillery unit in the same division. Only later did more soldiers from the army join them. Kampf said that news of the slaughter came to him only in the morning of the next day, and that he reported it immediately to the Central Command of the Land Forces and asked that an investigation be made against those responsible. In the afternoon of September 7 the army commander arrived at the division headquarters and met with all the unit commanders under Kampf. The commander denounced the act unequivocally, accusing the commanders of being unethical, uncultured and without honor. He further accused them of beastly behavior, saying that the deed had stained the honor of the whole division in the worst possible way. His words suggested that the head executors of the crime must receive the death penalty for their actions. During the trial more witnesses supported this testimony of Küchler's behavior.

Another document which was used as evidence in the Nurenberg trial no. 12 was the war journal of General Franz Halder, chief of staff of the land forces. He also mentioned the murder of the Krasnosielc Jews: "Artillerymen from the SS armored unit put Jews in synagogues and murdered them. A military court found the murderers guilty and sentenced them to one year in prison. Küchler refused to authorize punishment because it was too light. It was suggested that the unit be transferred instead." As a result of the publication of Halder's war journal the incident received widespread publicity and resonance in Germany.

In spite of the great excitement I felt at the document's exposure, I was still bothered by the question of where the victims of the slaughter were buried. The documents stated that the bodies were moved to an unknown location. Although I had come a long way in uncovering what had happened, I knew that until I answered that particular riddle, I would know no peace of mind.

To gather the funds needed to finance the continuing investigation, I established an operation committee in 1993. This committee had three members apart from myself, all descendants of Krasnosielc natives – Avi Golnder, Nathan Blenkitni and Zvika Knafi. An American lawyer by the name of Ed Faser also came to our aid, since his parents had lived in the town in the '20s before they immigrated to the United States. Ed Faser linked me with former townspeople in the United States, and they helped me raise more funds for the investigation.

Despite the enthusiasm of committee members and other former townspeople, many of them doubted the investigation was really worthwhile since they assumed the Poles would obstruct all channels of information. Others said that history cannot be changed in any case, and even if we succeed in erecting a memorial, the anti-Semitic Poles would only tear it down. These arguments did not weaken my resolve, and I insisted upon continuing the investigation. I decided to approach people at the German embassy in Israel and ask them to help finance the project.

Meanwhile, in 1993 I ran into some good luck meeting a Polish couple, both journalists, named Grazyna and Przemyslaw Rejer, who provided significant assistance in researching the affair. The Rejar couple, owners and publishers of a Polish economic newspaper, came to Israel to try and market the paper to Polish-speaking Israelis. A lawyer who knew me via some business connection suggested they should meet me. We all had dinner in my house, during which the two Poles complained that Holocaust survivors are hostile toward the Poles for allegedly aiding the Germans, while in truth there is a large measure of perversion of history in that belief. They argued that most of the Polish people did not cooperate with the Germans but suffered greatly under the yoke of the German occupation. I replied that the Poles were antagonistic toward me during the war and even after it was over. I told them of my numerous attempts at enlisting the aid of the mayor of Krasnosielc, of his adamant refusal to allow me access to the town archives; of the cold shoulder the townspeople showed me when I asked them to help me find the mass grave of my father and his friends.

"If the Poles do not want to help me commemorate the dead," I said, "how can one speak of friendly relations among the living?" The Rejar couple listened attentively to my words. Mrs. Rejar promised me she would take care of the matter and that she and her husband would spare no effort in helping us. She promised to use all of their contacts in the media and the government to lend us a hand.

I remained in telephone communication with them, and at the end of the year I received a letter: "You have a place to go to, to recite Kaddish on your father's grave," the letter stated. "We found one of the elder townsmen, a Mr. Zielinski, and he testified that he took part in burying and covering up the bodies on the night of the slaughter."

It turned out that in that same year the Rejar couple had published an article in the paper, in which they requested their readers to send them any information concerning Krasnosielc's Jews. Furthermore, they drove all the way to Krasnosielc from their hometown Poznan, a distance of two hundred eighty miles, especially to gather eyewitness accounts. They went from door to door, asking everyone, and did not stop until they came to a woman named Mrs. Kolkovaska, the sister of my former teacher, who gave them the information they were seeking. The woman said that one of the town's residents, a man by the name of Marian Zielinski, knew where the bodies were buried. Zielinski lived close to the synagogue. On the night of the slaughter the Germans knocked on his door and ordered him to come and help cover up the bodies.

I joined the couple in Poland and together we went to interview Mr. Zielinski. I interrogated him formally in the Town Council building, and the mayor functioned as a witness. I had Mr. Zielinski sign a document stating that he was telling the truth, and nothing but the truth, since his testimony would be used as evidence in a court of law. And indeed, Mr. Zielinski testified that one evening in September 1939 (he refused to commit to a specific date) he witnessed the burial of Jewish bodies close to the town's synagogue. He was apparently afraid to testify that he had covered the bodies himself, perhaps because he feared being held responsible for the murder. Afterwards I went with Mr. Zielinski and his son to the burial site next to the synagogue, and he showed me exactly where the bodies were interred.

Zielinski said in his testimony that he was a witness to the removal of the bodies from the synagogue by the Germans. He described how they were thrown into nearby ditches. The Germans then covered the dead with Bibles they found inside the synagogue, poured fuel over them, and ignited them. The Germans then called on him and his father to help cover up the bodies. Immediately afterwards they warned them that should they ever speak of what they saw, they and their families' lives would be forfeited. Only after the war could Mr. Zielinski unburden himself of the horrible secret, and thus the rumor spread in town until it came to our ears. The couple publicized the new facts in their paper *Przeglad Handlowy* (Market review), which was printed in their hometown of Poznan. In 1995, a year after he gave his account, Mr. Zielinski passed away, and I felt that divulging the truth had somewhat relieved him of his part in the terrible murder.

Now that I had the proof that the bodies were buried next to the synagogue, I considered beginning the process of opening the grave and exhuming the bodies. However, the Polish Health Department and the Polish Pathological Institute refused to authorize my request. Eventually we acquired the approval of a few rabbis to treat the site as an authorized graveyard in every respect, and we gave up the excavation. Meanwhile Mr. Galinka, the mayor of Krasnosielc, finally decided to cooperate with me. This change in his attitude was mainly due to the journalists' support, and because formal bodies, such as the Polish Bureau of Foreign Affairs and the Polish Health Department, had become involved. He permitted me access to the synagogue building and the Krasnosielc archives, but to my consternation I found no evidence related to the actual execution of the Jews.

I then decided to erect a memorial to the victims of the incident. I approached the mayor and suggested that a library or museum be established on the site. He considered the idea and offered to sell me the synagogue building for a sum of twenty-five thousand dollars, and then I could do what I wanted with it. Mrs. Rejar was excited about the idea of buying the synagogue. She offered to establish an association dedicated to raising the one hundred thousand dollars needed to buy and renovate the building. Mrs. Rejar also made it clear that she would volunteer to be CEO of this association. My friends and confidantes in the committee again expressed serious doubts as to the possibility of raising such a sum. I approached the German Embassy in Israel and inquired if they would be willing to participate in such a project. The Germans stipulated their assistance on the condition that we present them a plan for the renovation of the building and its maintenance in the future. However, in an examination made by an Israeli engineer the building was determined to be very old, and due to its poor infrastructure it was inadvisable to invest money in it. This assessment eliminated the plan for me as well, and so I decided on a different option instead: building a memorial site. The mayor of Krasnosielc gave the new initiative his blessing. Meanwhile I continued in my efforts to try and raise funds for the project in different ways. Among other things I approached the staff of Yad Vashem, but I left them empty-handed. I visited the Wiesenthal Center in Los Angeles and the Holocaust Museum in Washington D.C. to learn how to build and maintain memorial sites. At the same time I sent out letters to survivors of the Krasnosielc slaughter asking for their involvement, but they could assist me only with very small amounts. One of the foundations I contacted agreed to donate funds on the condition that I operate as a legally registered committee. In order to set up such a committee I would need an entire apparatus (accounting, annual meetings, routine auditing and so forth) which would require further financing. I felt that I simply didn't have the energy to take such measures.

Eventually, salvation came from none other than the German Embassy in Israel. The cultural attaché of the embassy, Dr. Susan Reiner, provided ample assistance and maintained contact with the Foundation for Allocation of Funds in the German Ministry of Foreign Affairs. She sent letters, recommendations and requests. She even organized two meetings in which the military attaché and the embassy's chief accountant were present. After many efforts the embassy approved a sum of twenty thousand dollars which was enough to partially cover the research expenses and the founding of the memorial site.

Since the project would be erected on Polish soil, I found out from the German Bureau of Foreign Affairs that according to the law they must donate the money to a formal Polish body of some sort. It became clear therefore that I could not collect the money in my name. Krasnosielc's council could not be trusted with the money, since they had a deficit at the time and I feared they would use it for their own purposes. I decided to refrain from letting them handle the matter and instead founded a committee in Poland. I approached Mr. Marjan Bark, Poland's consul in Israel, and he connected me with a businessman in Warsaw. Together we founded a committee and called it Arca (Ark), based on the story of Noah's ark which tells how remnants from the deluge were save. This name symbolized for us the commemoration of remnants of the Jewish culture in the Makov district. The executive board of the committee consisted of Marjan Bark, the mayor of Krasnosielc, the mayor of Makov, three additional friends and myself. The function of the committee was to transfer to us the money to build the monument. I traveled to Warsaw twice especially to write the committee's regulations. Among other things I determined in the regulations my control over allocation of funds. I also visited the German Embassy in Warsaw to hasten transfer of the grant. I was aided in my quest by the embassy's press secretary, Mr. Steinline, and also by a Dr. Helga Hirsch, a journalist for the German newspaper *Frankfurter Allgemeine Zeitung*, who came to Poland to research German behavior during the occupation. I contacted the journalist, and since we didn't get to meet in Poland, I traveled to Germany. We met in Berlin and talked about the Krasnosielc slaughter at length. Two years later, on May 24, 1997, she published an extensive article on the subject in her newspaper.

During that time we continued working on plans for the memorial site. On the external wall of the synagogue we decided to install plaques in four languages – Hebrew, Yiddish, English and Polish – and each would contain a description of the slaughter that occurred there. In addition, a hundred yards from the synagogue building, in the place where the bodies were buried, we decided to erect a tombstone shaped like the two tablets of the Ten Commandments on which there would be inscribed the details of the incident in Hebrew and Polish, as well as the names of those murdered.

To achieve this I had to compile a list of the names of the victims, and this was no easy task. Nowhere could we find an organized census of the names, and we weren't even sure of their number. We knew that in addition to the people of the town, there were refugees from nearby towns buried there as well. In the Polish documents forty-one victims were mentioned, while the German reports mentioned fifty. With the help of a few former townspeople in the United States, among them my brothers and sisters, we succeeded in reconstructing a list of thirty-one names of people that we definitively knew were buried there, and a few additional names of Jews who had lived in the town, but we weren't certain if they were actual victims of the crime. Afterwards, with the help of the Soldiers Commemoration Unit of the Ministry of Defense, I had the names of the murdered inscribed on the tablets in both Hebrew and Polish. Then we fixed the tablets on the tombstone. The four plaques which were hung on the synagogue wall were designed by a Polish architect named Wojciech Henrykowski.

Twenty-five former townspeople gathered in Krasnosielc for the unveiling ceremony. Fifteen of us were from Israel – my brother Aharon and myself among them – and ten more from the United States. On June 5, 1996, the official event took place. Almost all the town's inhabitants came to the ceremony. There were also representatives of nearby towns. The presence of the people of Krasnosielc imparted great significance to the event and Israeli flags were flown along all the streets. An orchestra provided musical accompaniment. Naturally, the event attracted a lot of media attention.

The ceremony was divided into two parts. The first took place next to the synagogue and included speeches by the local district mayor, the town mayor, the deputy ambassador of Israel in Warsaw and Dina Rott, chairperson of Israel's committee concerning Polish regional towns. I translated the speeches into Polish and English. My own address, about my childhood memories from the town and the need and desire to investigate the incident, closed the first stage of the ceremony.

In the second part of the ceremony we marched toward the tombstone, to the place where the bodies were buried. There, my brother Aharon conducted the prayer, and we all recited Kaddish and psalms with him. Fifty-seven years had elapsed since the day I saw my father for the last time. I knew he was murdered and buried somewhere unknown. And now, finally, the moment came when I could close the circle and recite Kaddish at his grave. Words fail to describe the emotion that overcame me during those moments. After the prayer was over flower garlands were laid on the tombstone from the deputy ambassador, the representative of the Ministry of Defense, the regional representative and the mayor.

Then we all entered the synagogue building, which had been cleaned and made ready for the occasion by the townspeople. The event was documented by many media people, and some of those present, myself among them, gave interviews to the local TV stations.

Around noon we returned to the guesthouse, where we met with a minister from the Polish government who was responsible for relations with the Jewish-Polish Diaspora throughout the world (he had been unable to arrive for the ceremony itself). The minister gave an hour-long speech, in which he mentioned the significance of commemoration and spoke of the relations between Jews and Poles.

In the years to come the Krasnosielc site received wide attention in Germany and Poland. A German production company making a film about war crimes committed by German soldiers in the beginning of the war documented the story of the Krasnosielc murders based on the facts I had uncovered. They even sent a crew to film the site. They wanted me to be interviewed for the film, but I was prevented from doing so because I was in the hospital at the time. The film was broadcast on one of the German TV stations, and later in Poland.

I felt a tremendous sense of accomplishment that this incident, which was of such personal significance to me, and which roused public and historic interest as well, had finally received its rightful place in the history books. It was the first act of mass murder committed by Germans in Poland, as well as the only time before the war's end when SS soldiers were put on trial for the murder of Jews.

* * *

With the erection of the Krasnosielc memorial one of my dreams had been realized, but the other was still unfulfilled – to commemorate the memory of the Jews who fell in battle against the Nazis. During the war I had already resolved that should I survive and come out of this hell alive,

I would commemorate the memory of the fallen Jews. I believed it was important to emphasize their contribution to victory, principally because Poland's formal military establishments hadn't done enough to call attention to the Jews' part in the fighting.

Around two hundred thousand Jewish soldiers served in Poland's armies during World War II. These Jewish soldiers belonged to three different components of the army, each operating in different areas and in different periods of the war.

When war broke out there were a hundred fifty thousand Jewish soldiers and fifty thousand Jewish officers serving in the Polish army. The officers were mostly doctors, engineers, economists and rabbis. Throughout the battles to defend Poland until its surrender at the end of September 1939, twenty thousand Jewish fighters were killed, captured or declared missing. Half of these fell while protecting Warsaw.

After Nazi Germany's invasion of Poland, the Polish government in exile established itself in London. Its instructions were that wherever there was suitable manpower for the task, new Polish military units should be established. In this way, Poland's fight against the Germans would continue. In France there were large communities of Polish immigrants, among whom there were many Jews. Some of them had volunteered to fight with the Republicans in the Spanish Civil war and had come to live in France after their downfall. The Polish army in France, founded on September 6, 1939, numbered fifteen thousand men and women. This army suffered heavy casualties while battling the Germans. Some of its fighters managed to escape into Britain via Dunkirk, while others joined the French MCI resistance. Many of them were killed or captured during the covert activities they carried out against the Germans.

Polish armies operated in the Soviet Union as well. After Poland was conquered in September 1939, many Polish soldiers retreated to eastern Poland. When the Molotov-Ribbentrop Pact came into effect, the majority of these Polish soldiers were imprisoned in Soviet POW camps. In 1940, a year before the German attack on the Soviet Union, the Soviet government committed atrocious acts of slaughter in Katyn. They cold-bloodedly murdered sixteen thousand Polish officers, among them roughly seven hundred Jews. Following political changes that occurred later, the surviving Polish prisoners became soldiers in the two Polish armies that were assembled within Soviet borders. These armies would later participate in the battles against the Germans.

The First Army, called the Anders Army after its commander, General Vladislav Anders, numbered approximately seventy thousand soldiers and officers, of whom four thousand were Jewish. Many of the Jews held officer rank. Most of the Jews serving in the Anders Army volunteered to join it out of their own initiative, as its anti-Semitic commanders didn't approve of recruiting Jews. In 1942 the Anders Army forces left the Soviet Union and joined the British command in the Middle East. They crossed the Soviet-Iranian border and continued into Iraq, and from there to Palestine. In the land of Israel most of the Jews abandoned the army and joined the Etzel, the Lechi and the Hagana – among them the future prime minister of Israel, Menachem Begin. Thanks to their technical and military capabilities, their contribution to the pre–Independence War fighting in Israel was especially significant. Many of them became the central pillars of the IDF, mainly in the armored forces, artillery and medical corps. The rest of the soldiers of the Anders Army, along with the one thousand Jews who didn't stay in Israel, continued to Europe. There, they participated in the bloody Monte Cassino battle and other battles along the Adriatic shore in Italy. Hundred of Jews were killed during these battles as well.

The Second Army, called The Polish People's Army, was established in 1943 as part of the Red Army, under the command of Colonel Zygmunt Berling. The army numbered approximately eighty thousand men – a quarter of them Jewish, and many of them officers in various command posts. I also served as a soldier among their ranks. The first trial by fire this army endured was the bloody battle by the village of Lenino (in Byelorussia of today). Sometime later the Polish People's Army helped liberate Poland from the hands of the Germans, and its soldiers fought all the way to Berlin. After the liberation many of the officers in this army were awarded high-ranking posts in the now liberated Poland. Approximately twelve hundred Jews were killed or declared missing during those battles. Many Jews who were former Polish People's Army soldiers later assisted Polish youth groups immigrating to Israel, and later immigrated themselves. They enlisted in the IDF and strengthened the ranks of the young Israeli army.

I felt that it was important to mark the contribution of these Polish-Jewish fighters and honor their deaths.

I took the first practical step in this matter in 1992, the evening of Ehud Barak's trip to Poland. As the current chief of staff Barak was traveling to Poland for the forty-fifth anniversary of the Warsaw Ghetto Uprising. I sent him a letter, in which I asked him to place a garland on the Unknown Polish Soldier's grave, in memory of the tens of thousands of Jewish soldiers who fell in the ranks of the Polish army. Barak answered that he couldn't do it in the planned trip, but a suitable opportunity for the state to commemorate them would be found.

In this early stage I realized that in order to build the prospective memorial I would need resources and administrative assistance. Based on my experience with erecting the Krasnosielc memorial, I also knew that in order to receive contributions I would need to do one of two things: found an association or join an existing association. The association had to be a nonprofit organization in order that we could avoid paying taxes on the contributions and so that the contributions would count as tax-deductible expenses. I decided in 1994 to join the Association of Polish Army Expatriates in Israel. The organization, founded that same year, made it its mission to commemorate the memory of the Jewish fighters in Poland's armies and to pass on their legacy to future generations. At the time of its founding the association did not operate in a nonprofit framework. When I presented the idea of erecting the monument to the organization's CEO he was unenthusiastic, claiming that he was too old for such an undertaking, and that he had neither the manpower nor the funds. I promised him that I would acquire financing myself, and asked if he could help me only by providing office services. The CEO agreed and suggested we organize a special committee with the goal of building the memorial, with only four members – the CEO, myself, the late Benjamin Ziegel and Haim Zussman.

At an early stage of the partnership the CEO already failed to keep his promise. He did not supply the administrative services I had asked for. He suggested I cover the expenses out of my own pocket. He explained that all my expenses would be repaid once the project was complete, out of the remaining donation funds. I did not find this suggestion satisfactory, and I was particularly disappointed that he made our project the lowest priority on the association's list. At that point I had already noticed that the CEO was mainly interested in the money my project would bring to his organization. The monument itself did not interest him. And so I had no choice but to work from my home and at my private expense. I purchased a computer, a fax machine and other office appliances, and through the subsequent months and years I devoted days, nights and innumerable resources to the cause. The personal monetary expense was tremendous, and Chaya had reason to protest more than once.

I held negotiations with various committees in the Ministry of Defense in an attempt to receive an allocation of funds for the monument and a site on which it could be erected. It was eventually decided that a plot would be allocated in Mount Herzl, between the memorial monuments for the men of the Jewish Brigade and for the two hundred thousand soldiers who died in the ranks of the Soviet military. The Ministry of Defense also promised to give additional aid and a fifty thousand shekel (roughly twelve thousand US dollars) grant for building expenses. They stipulated that the sum would be transferred only after additional sponsors were found. Their official reason was that it must not appear as though they were the sole supporters of any given body. At their recommendation we approached an architect who had planned several monuments on Mount Herzl, and we even received from him a draft for the monument's construction. The cost of such a project was estimated at four hundred thousand shekels (about one hundred thousand US dollars). During several months I tried to gather the aforementioned sum, meeting with representatives of various bodies who had shown sympathy for the idea, but they refused to make a donation as long as the committee wasn't registered as a nonprofit organization. Unfortunately, the CEO of the Association of Polish Army Expatriates, who was supposed to have been working toward registering the committee as a nonprofit organization, was remiss in his responsibilities. I had a feeling he had "psychological inhibitions," and that he was playing petty games of respect and jealousy with me. Eventually, however, I overcame all obstacles and the project started moving. Actions and events that took place afterwards proved my feelings and fears to be true.

In 1995, when I found that the matter of the nonprofit organization was being delayed, I traveled to the United States to gather funds from various contributors. I found a certain organization which was willing to donate on the condition that my committee registers itself as a nonprofit organization according to the American standards. However, at that time

I had not even been able to convince the CEO to register according to the Israeli standards, which were much less strict. I returned to Israel in bitter disappointment, but I insisted on soldiering on. I remained steadfast in my determination to complete the journey that I had begun. By this time I had come to see it as a sacred quest.

One day the CEO informed me that he had approached the heads of the Associations of Polish Army Expatriates in England and that they were willing to donate fifteen thousand pounds sterling to the project. A few times he traveled to England to supposedly collect the money, while at the same time financing his trips with the organization's funds. In hindsight I discovered that the organizations in England promised to make the donation only after construction was complete. A sum of three thousand English pounds that was received as an advance were declared by him to be intended for remembrance books which he was authoring, not for the monument at all. I noticed the irregularities in the association's management, and I considered reporting them. Eventually, so as not to sabotage the project, I decided to ignore the irregularities and continue in my efforts to obtain grants. Meanwhile, the years progressed and the Ministry of Defense threatened to withdraw its offerings should we fail to execute the plan in a reasonable period of time.

And just when I believed we were not going to be successful, a breakthrough occurred. In the middle of 1997 I met a Mr. Sami Shamoon in the Polish embassy. He was a Jew of Iraqi descent and of considerable means. Shamoon was based in London, and lived both in London and in Israel. His personal representative for his business in Israel was Mr. Meir Dekel. Mr. Shamoon cared deeply about issues of commemoration. Among other causes, he donated money for the construction of a monument for the soldiers who served in the Intelligence Corps. After a few meetings Mr. Shamoon agreed to finance 50 percent of the cost of the monument to the Polish Jewish soldiers. His reason for doing so was especially moving and unusual. The meeting's protocol preserved Mr. Shamoon's words: "Mr. Sami Shamoon expressed his reservations about the way things work, the fact that each ethnic group commemorates only its own dead. 'This matter,' Shamoon emphasized, 'belongs to all of Israel, and requires cooperation among all ethnic groups.' He desired to break this circle of separation. While a member of the Babylonian ethnic group himself, he wished to participate in an enterprise to commemorate the Jews from Poland's armies, who died in their battle against the Nazis."

With his donation Mr. Shamoon wished to pay his respects to the Jewish soldiers of the Anders army, also known by its formal name, the Second Polish Corpus, who joined the eighth British camp in the years 1942–43, in order to fight against the Nazis in the west. These soldiers trekked through the Soviet Union, Iran and Iraq on their way to Palestine. They aspired to reach the West African Desert or Italy. During their stay in Iran and especially in Iraq, they were received hospitably by the local Jewish communities.

I felt that we were finally making headway. I introduced Sami Shamoon to Mr. Naaman Schaiek, who was responsible for the commemoration issue in the Ministry of Defense, and they signed an agreement. Mr. Shamoon was willing to begin transferring the money. At the same time I asked the CEO to open a separate account for the monument construction project and activate inspection routines as the law requires, but he did not comply. His reasons were varied but they did not ring true. I explained to him that Mr. Shamoon has shown his determination to contribute to the project. I made clear to him that the Ministry of Defense was also involved and that they are pressuring us to move this matter forward. It was of no use. The CEO persisted in his stubborn refusal.

Meanwhile I was urged to advance by Mr. Schaiek as well as Mr. Shamoon, who couldn't comprehend why the monument's account had not as yet been opened. I hesitated to tell him about the CEO's reservations, fearing that the sponsors might withdraw their assistance. I preferred talking about bureaucratic difficulties. As a result Mr. Shamoon accused me of reneging on my promises. Needless to say, this caused me great anxiety. Eventually he decided to open a separate account, and from it he paid the contractor who began building the monument. He even promised the contractor that he would cover all the expenses himself. I, for my part, promised to reimburse him for all the money he spent in excess of the sum for which he committed himself, as soon as more donations arrive.

In the beginning of 1998, construction of the monument was completed. At that stage the CEO suddenly introduced himself as the sole person responsible for the project. Among other things he traveled to Poland to report the monument's construction, and he even asked the Polish Defense

Ministry for a present in his honor: the forging of a large eagle. The eagle that was forged was placed at the entrance to the monument square. He also invited the CEO of the Association of Polish Army Expatriates in England to come and see the finished monument, but he refrained from introducing me to him. The donation which was received after the visit did not end up in the monument account.

Meanwhile the Ministry of Defense transferred a check for the sum of fifty thousand shekels, as promised. The check was written to the Association of Polish Army Expatriates, but since the organization was not registered as nonprofit, twenty thousand shekels were immediately deducted by income tax, as required by law. This enraged me. We could have easily saved that sum if the CEO had only legally registered the association as a nonprofit organization.

At this stage we were still seventy-five thousand shekels short of covering the project's expenses. I decided to approach an old friend of mine for a donation, Mr. Yossi Maimon, owner of the Merchav Hashkaot company. Mr. Maimon's father had served in the Polish army. He replied that he would only agree to donate if he receives a receipt from a nonprofit organization. I forwarded this request to the project committee, and again came up against the CEO's furtiveness. Finally, I approached Mr. Ze'ev Bar, CEO of the Yad Labanim organization in Jerusalem – a certified nonprofit organization. I met with Mr. Maimon's authorized representative, and he wrote the check to the Yad Labanim organization, and was given the proper receipt. The money was later transferred to the monument account. As I mentioned before, I did everything in my power to make this project succeed, while the CEO did nothing but hamper it.

The entire sum which accumulated in Sami Shamoon's account was transferred to the contractor who built the monument. The reimbursement I was promised by the CEO was supposed to come from donations of sponsors in London. And yet, in spite of all the promises made to me, only half of my personal expenses for this project were reimbursed. All my attempts to regain the rest were refused. I found some consolation in the fact that I had succeeded in gathering many donations for the monument.

Everything was made ready for the monument's opening ceremony. And then, a week before the ceremony, the CEO approached the Ministry of Defense, obstinately requesting that my name not be written as the project's initiator beside the names of the sculptor, contractor, and sponsors. This, despite the fact that I initiated the entire project, and recruited all the sponsors.

On October 26, 1998, the monument unveiling ceremony took place at the military cemetery on Mount Herzl. Among those present were the presiding minister of defense, Mr. Yitshak Mordechai, the Polish minister of defense, the Polish minister in charge of World War II veteran affairs (an important formal position in Poland), Poland's ambassador to Israel, a Polish honor guard made up of approximately thirty Polish officers and soldiers from the UN forces stationed on the Golan Heights and a group of IDF soldiers. Also participating in the ceremony were military attachés from the embassies of England, New Zealand and Italy, as well as a small group of war veterans from the armies of Poland and Russia. Sami Shamoon, serving as CEO of the Sephardic Federation in London and CEO of the Center for Babylonia's Legacy, invited dozens of Babylonian Jews. Among them were representatives of Shas, Israel's Orthodox Sephardic political party. And of course, my family was present as well. All in all, there were approximately five hundred people, with a substantial number of dignitaries from both Israel and countries abroad.

In the course of the impressive ceremony there were speeches made by the minister of defense, Yitshak Mordechai, by representatives of the Polish government, and by the CEO of the Polish Emigrants' Association. Rabbi Pinchas Rozengarten recited chapters from Psalms. He had served as a military rabbi in the Anders Army and had presided over the burial of the Jewish dead after the battle of Monte Cassino. I, too, addressed the crowd. Witnessing the fulfillment of my cherished dream moved me unspeakably, and my words came directly from my heart.

CHAPTER THIRTEEN

In Retirement

The efforts that I had invested in erecting the two monuments and the pressures that I had had to deal with had a negative effect on my health. I suffered from attacks of shortness of breath, and my doctor advised me not to exert myself. As a result, Chaya and I moved to a new apartment in Ramat Gan, where we have lived since 1994.

At the end of 1998 I was hospitalized and underwent a complicated heart operation. The hospitalization and recovery took about a year. I had a great deal of time on my hands and I reflected on my way in life, especially the events that had preceded the building of the memorial. My wife Chaya had asked me some sharp questions at the time. "Should it be at any price…?" she would challenge me. But I had not had answers for her.

After I recovered I returned as in the years preceding the operation to devote most of my time and energy to public activity. Upon the completion of the two large projects that I had been instrumental in establishing – the memorial for the victims of the murder at Krasnoscielc and the memorial for the Jews who fell in the service of the Polish Armies, I became busy with other activities, mostly in the public area. In addition, I began to document my past and continued to be active in issues related to commemoration.

During most of my time as a resident of Ramat Gan I was active in the Rotary Club in that city. Twice I served as president of the club. The

Rotary initiated various projects benefiting the city's needy, including the *Anush* Club for mentally disturbed children, a club for the treatment of alcoholism and study grants for needy youth. I was counted among the founders and instructors of the Rotaract – the young body of the Rotary movement, which was aimed at people aged seventeen to thirty who were intended to be the future generation of the movement. However, after I left these functions, no one could be found to replace me and the club remained without a leader to carry on. It soon stopped functioning and was eventually dissolved.

Besides all these activities, I am often invited to give lectures at schools, homes for the elderly and in other frameworks, mainly on the subject of memorials and commemoration. I enjoy lecturing immensely, and feel satisfaction from the fact that the audience usually takes an interest in the subject and in my lectures.

Now and again I write articles – including an essay I penned for the Rotary Club's magazine and an article for Givat Chaviva's *Yalkut Moreshet* (Heritage Anthology) concerning the massacre at Krasnoscielc.

I am a member of many associations: the Palmach Generation Association, the Machal International Committee, the Museum of the Jewish Fighters in World War II (where I represent the Machal International Committee), the Yad Vashem Council, the Association of Veterans of Polish Armies in World War II, the Navy Association, the Communication Association, the Organization of Former Residents of Krasnoscielc, the Higher Committee of Beer-Sheva, the Association of Towns of North Mazovia in Poland, the Association of Academics of the Humanities and Society, the Retirees Organization of the IAI and the Association for Research on the Defense Force of Israel. Up to this day I engage in various activities connected with these associations.

I take special care to stay in touch with friends who served in the past as managers of various agencies in Kiryat Shmona, and we meet once a month and discuss various subjects.

Chaya gave up her activities as mentor for Yachad in 1995, and since then has integrated successfully in various activities. She visits museums and galleries and maintains political and social involvement, including volunteering in the Welfare Division of Ramat Gan. She also meets regularly with family and friends and attends various classes.

We maintain contacts with most of our friends from the various periods of our life – from the days of our freedom in Haifa, through our residence in Kiryat Shmona and our sojourns in Italy. And the same holds true for our friends from the different companies I worked for.

After the Zionist Forum called for Israeli families to adopt immigrant families to help in their absorption in Israel, we decided in 1990 to adopt an immigrant family from the former Soviet Union. Chaya, who was active in various volunteer agencies, was asked if she could adopt a family from Kiev. Without too much internal struggle we decided together to respond to the challenge. The Skvirsky family, Valentina (Valia) and Alex and their two girls, Helena and Anna, rented an apartment in the Yad Eliahu neighborhood. Valia quickly found work in a store in the shopping center of Ramat Aviv, where she continues to work to this day. Alex was trained as a television technician in Kiev and we found him work as a technician at the Amcor Company. Since that was not entirely successful I looked for other places of work for him. In the end he retrained and began to work as a maintenance technician in the surgery rooms of Ichilov Hospital, where he works to this day. Helena found work in the office of a certified accountant and Anna married a young man from Jaffa. In time they were joined by their third daughter Svetlana and her two children. Svetlana is now taking a nursing course at Tel Hashomer.

For years we helped members of the Skvirsky family in various ways, from small material help such as gifts of electric appliances that we didn't need anymore to guidance and social support. We went touring with them to different places in the country and invited them to the Purim party organized by the rotary. We celebrated Alex's birthday at a restaurant with the whole family. And every year we celebrate the Passover seder with them in our home. With time their situation is improving and they need less and less of our help, but we maintain friendly relations with them.

Now and again Chaya and I vacation at various locations here in Israel and abroad. From time to time we go for a few days' vacation with our three sons and their families to different sites in Israel, such as Maalot and Kibbutz Hagoshrim.

Chaya and I are proud of our children, who are considerate, honest and good-hearted. Over the years each one acquired a profession and a family of his own.

All my life I have tried to maintain as close relations as possible with my brothers and sisters who have spread out to different countries. My family is very dear to me and despite the physical distance separating us and the different ways of life that we chose for ourselves we maintain close ties as we each, in our own ways, try to preserve the tradition that our parents of blessed memory bequeathed to us.

◆ ◆ ◆

Appendix

Curriculum Vitae for David Shachar

Name: David Shachar
Marital Status: Married + 3 children
Place of Birth: Krasnosielc, Poland

Present Address: 116 Uziel St. Ramat Gan 52302
Telephone: 03-5732348
Fax: 03-5732348
E-mail: sh_david@internet-zahav.net

1935–39: Study in heder and Polish elementary school

1939–45: Under German occupation and in far north of the Soviet Union (1943–45: Volunteer in the Polish People's Army)

1945–46: Underwent training in kibbutz in Poland in preparation for immigration to Palestine

1946–48: Studied radio-electronics, Paris

1948–49: Volunteered for Machal in Independence War (Negev Brigade of Palmach and Communication Corps)

1950–1958: Various occupations in field of electronics (Ministry of Defense, Training and Maintenance)

1958–67: Volunteer for development town of Kiryat Shmona (in "City to Border" program). Established technical service center in Kiryat Shmona, taught and trained youth in technical professions, organized independent business, acted as managing director of the Kiryat Shmona Development Company)

1967–82: Israeli Aircraft Corporation Ltd. (Development, design, training, technical documentation)

1971–76: Representative of Israeli Aircraft Corporation and Ministry of Defense in Europe

1977–82: European Marketing desk, Israeli Aircraft Corporation

1982–85: Managing director of engineering company in Europe

1985–88: Independent business activities in Israel and abroad (technical translations, ecology, etc.)

1988–96: Volunteer activities devoted to investigation of first mass murder of Jews in Poland, which took place on September 5, 1939. Established a memorial at the scene of the massacre in the town of Krasnosielc near Warsaw.

1992–98: Establishment of memorial for 30,000 Jewish soldiers who fell in the service of Polish armies in World War II. Memorial located at the Military Cemetery on Mount Herzl in Jerusalem.

1998–Present: Writing biography and documentation of memorial activities that I carried out.

PUBLIC ACTIVITIES

Active member of Rotary movement from 1960. Active on behalf of Academics Association, Palmach Association, Polish Immigrants Association and five other associations.

EDUCATION

Electronic technician, Paris, France

Bar Ilan University: BA in Economics, Sociology and Jewish Studies

Tel Aviv University: Courses in Management and Business Administration, toward MBA (degree not completed)

Courses and further studies in electronics, computers, management, languages and others.

HONORS

Appointed member of the Yad Vashem Council

Histadrut Year 2000 award presented at the Ramat Gan/Bnei Brak branch

Medals for participation in Israel campaigns, Defense, Independence War, Sinai Campaign, Six-Day War, Yom Kippur War

Two decorations awarded by the Polish Government

LANGUAGES

Hebrew, English, Yiddish, Italian, French, Polish and Russian (at various levels)

The Murder of the Jews of Krasnosielc

An extract from the verdict of the German military court for the murders at the synagogue (September 14, 1939)

The head of the military court announced by telephone: A field court of the armored division Kempf sentenced an SS man from the SS artillery to three years imprisonment for murder, and nine years imprisonment with hard labor for a corporal of the military police.

Both murdered about 50 Jews who were taken for a day to repair a bridge. After finishing work they were confined during the evening in the synagogue and there shot to death without any reason.

General Alder wishes to know the judgment of the 3rd Army command.

The judgment was passed on to the commander of the 3rd Army for approval. The demand of the representative of the prosecution: Sentence of death for murder.

[The judgment on the day after the deed:]
To:
Headquarters of the Land Forces,
Headquarters of the General Staff
Sa13/9
The observers are SS men

14.9.39

The head of Headquarters of the Land Forces requests that the document H 14/9) be returned to the Headquarters of the Land Forces.

I.A. Radke

* * *

SECRET
Telegram : HD1H 403 14.9. 39 1905

To the consultant to the Higher Military Court at the Head of the General Staff in Berlin

Tirpitzufer 72-76, Berlin W35.

Su9bjecxt AZ480
General Staff Room 3 Headquarters of the Land Force No. 1204/39

We recognized in the discussion relating to the SS soldier mitigating circumstances because passing the rifle by an officer into his hands deviated him from taking an active part in the execution by rifle fire. He was in an emotional state due to the many terrible deeds carried out by the Poles toward Germans. He, as an SS man, in seeing the Jews felt especially the anti-German attitude of the Jews and in youthful excitement acted without thinking in advance. He is a good soldier and has no previous convictions.

The councillor of the Higher Military Court of the Lands Forces approves the correctness of the document.

Lipsky
Advisor to the Military Court

* * *

To: General Staff of the 3rd Division
Note: By telephone from the Head Advisor of the the Military Court the secretariat at the General Staff apparently will not approve the two judgments.

[Summary: The sentences were cut after the pardon.]

The punishments before the pardon and after the pardon:

Nine years in jail with hard labor for military police corporal, was reduced to three years in jail.

Three years in jail for SS man. Not changed.

Approved by the General Staff

Letter from Haim Himmelfarb

A letter sent by David Shachar's father to Yosef in July 23, 1937, telling him about the birth of Elimelech.

With God's help on this Sabbath evening I will ask for help in a small matter here in Krasnosielc. Life and peace and good luck to my beloved, my dear son who is that important young man Mr. Mordechai Yosef (may his light shine) Himmelfarb and to my dear uncle, our teacher and rabbi Dov Cohen (may his light shine), with good luck and much love. We, blessed be the Lord, who are alive and living in peace send you good news that your mother has given birth to a son with good luck and with the help of the Lord. I will circumcise him and he is well. May God give good luck to the family and I will have the good fortune to raise the fruit of my loins in the Torah and he will marry and do good deeds and bring satisfaction with wealth and happiness. Your mother is well and may God help and bless her and send her good health. The circumcision will be in Warsaw today. I have just come and I am writing you in haste because I am very tired from the traveling and suffered much distress in Warsaw but thank God everything turned out all right for us. May God let me hear from you. You haven't answered me any word about the good news card I wrote to you about the bad feeling I had.

Excuse me for the short time remaining, I will close with greeting from the whole family and if God grants I will write a longer letter. Your mother will also write.

Greeting from your father who wishes you well with love and is waiting for your answer.

Your father,
Haim Himmelfarb, *Shohet*

[The letter continues on the other side of the postcard:]
Your little brother is circumcised and asks that you write him and he wishes you well and thanks you. His name, may he have a long life, is Elimelech Benjamin, blessed be the Lord.

[Yosef's answer, as David heard it from his brother Michael:]
My longing to see the newborn is like that of Yosef for Binyamin.

Appendix

Letter from Yehoshua (Shaiki) Gavish, Chairman, Dor Hapalmach

To
David Shachar
116 Uziel St.
Ramat Gan 52302

January 6, 2003

Dear David,

I read your book with great interest.

    A great chapter in your life began at your home in Poland. The horrors of the Holocaust and the fate of your family, your mobilization into the Polish army, your volunteering and leaving for Israel, and your mobilization for the Palmach – the French Commando, the 8th Regiment, Nirim, the Independence War, the many duties in the North and at Kiryat Shmona, and volunteering for public organizations – I am filled with admiration for what you experienced and your activities.

    I passed your essay on to our archives.

    My congratulations on your activities, and I wish you full health so that you can continue them.

Sincerely yours,

Yehoshuah Gavish
Chairman
Dor Hapalmach

Dor Hapalmach: Registered Association No. 56-095-5644
10 Lebanon St. Tel Aviv, P.O..B. 65030, T.A. 91850
Tel. 03-6438460, 03-6418484 Fax 03-6414716

The Projects of the Kiryat Shmona Development Company

An article published in the newspaper Davar *(January 1965)*

The Kiryat Shmona Development Company was founded in 1955 upon the initiative of Ehud Avriel with the purpose of initiating and setting up projects that could contribute to the development of Kiryat Shmona, both economically (places of employment, stores, workshops and other services) and with regard to entertainment (cafés, movies and hotels, etc.).

The initiative was based on the assumption that without public initiative these projects would not get started. Still, the public aspect wasn't in the direction of profits. The policy was to initiate and then to encourage private groups who could continue to develop the object.

The first stockholders were: the Local Council (45%); The Workers Council (49%); the Regional Council (15%); with a starting capital of 50,000 lira. The businesses that were established by the company and that made a mark on Kiryat Shmona were:

1. Hula Textiles: A plant employing 399 workers was transferred to the Moller Group–Tiyus (the losses of the company totaled about 25,000 lira).
2. Swimming pool: This was transferred to the Local Council (loss to the company: 10,000 lira).
3. Hambro: Shopping center, banks and café were transferred to private interests under easy conditions.
4. Movie house: The movie house was built and is still in operation today. In partnership and profit with private investors under Elimelch Biederman.
5. Hotel Pe'er: The hotel was well known to travelers. It was transferred to private interests.
6. Sewing workshop: The sewing workshop passed through a number of changes until it was transferred to Mr. Shokrin, one of the workers there. The workshop employs 50–60 people and makes a decent profit margin (losses of the company: 25,000 lira).
7. Transfer of workshop owners and their improvement with the help of the government in building and with loans. Two centers were established: a workshop center and an industrial center for rehabilitation of a number of workshop owners in various trades.

Some additional experiments were tried to establish workplaces, but these failed with heavy losses to the company. The most outstanding of these was a diamond polishing plant in partnership with private interests which didn't succeed and the plant was closed with heavy losses. The company is now busy with two additional objects. The first project is a new, elegant hall with 1,100 seats for plays and concerts. In operating this we are witnessing a sight that has never been seen before – namely, the mobilization of private capital: eight participants for a sum of 250,000 lira invested in the cinema.

The importance of this investment is in the confidence the owners of these savings have in the development and advancement of Kiryat Shmona and its economic future and the loyalty of those who are engaged in its establishment.

The second project is a hotel, which has been established at a central location. It is modern and boasts a cellar-nightclub and first-class restaurant for 300 persons. This is intended for internal and foreign tourism which flows to the Upper Galilee during every holiday and especially during the summer months.

Two years ago changes took place in the ownership of the company with the entrance of Solel Boneh as a main partner. Partnership between the company and the implementation of most of the development plans with Solel Boneh has proved itself easy and efficient for the good of Kiryat Shmona.

Future plans:

Today emphasis is placed on the integration of Kiryat Shmona on the tourist map of the Upper Galilee. In addition to the hotel which is now in an advanced stage of construction the idea has been raised of operating a cable between Kiryat Shmona and the Naphtali Mountains. There is also an idea which is in the final planning stages of development of the Jungle – an area covered with tropical vegetation the length of the Ayun River, which has a good topography for camping, entertainment and holidaying. These projects, however, require major investment. But the company is considering them seriously, given the fact that they have the capacity to change the face of Kiryat Shmona from an economic and social standpoint.

Letter from the Ministry of Defense

Ministry of Defense / Rehabilitation Division
Soldier's Memorial Unit

April 27, 1998
Telephone: 03-6934401
CB/313/7

David Shachar
116 Uziel St.
Ramat Gan

I would like to express my utmost admiration for your action in memorializing the memory of 50 residents of Krasnosielc in Poland who were murdered by the Nazi beast and buried in a common grave in the courtyard of the synagogue.

In my visit to the town of Krasnosielc on April 21, 1998, I was able to see the common grave and pray there for their souls and also I was rewarded to see the synagogue where those murdered maintained their spiritual lives.

I have no doubt that this project will remain a memorial site for pilgrimage by Jews and non-Jews who believe in freedom and justice.

May their memory be blessed.

Naaman Schiek
Unit head

Letter from Mordecai Peltzur

Mordecai Peltzur
Shderot Ben-Zvi 39
Jerusalem 96260
Tel 02-6258035
Fax 02-6249669

To: Mr. David Shachar
116 Uziel St.
Ramat Gan 52302

Jerusalem 22.2.99

My very dear Mr. Shachar,

The purpose of my letter is to salute you, soldier to soldier, and by this to tender my feelings of sincere admiration for your part in the great project of the establishment of a memorial in memory of Jewish soldiers who gave their lives in the service of Polish armies, a memorial which was established because of your efforts, your perseverance and your persistence on Mount Herzl in Jerusalem, the capital city of Israel.

    I wish you to know that during your speech at the unveiling ceremony, your words not only excited me but also caused me to shudder. In listening to you on the prophecy of Ezekiel a column of images of people I knew passed before my eyes, people who fell in battles and whose graves are spread over three continents.

    Often I have wondered about the part of Polish Jews in the establishment of the state and all that preceded it, how all these things are beginning to be forgotten and reduced from their original importance. Generations come and generations go and what happened fifty, sixty or seventy years ago becomes a chapter in history in which few are interested. I can make this judgment since I remember what they did and what positions they occupied and what percentage of the Polish Jewry there was when I arrived in Israel in 1943. And the truth is that my heart is saddened at present when all this is not reflected in today's reality. I do not wish to blame anyone that the world and situations have changed and that in the meantime there have been residues of ill will and periods of being cut of from Poland – and these certainly have made their impact.

Personally my feelings on this subject are mixed, since my father, Professor Alexander Peltzur, of blessed memory, was a captain in the Polish army and during his service fought for the independence of Poland in World War I and was called to the flag upon the outbreak of war in September 1939, and in the end was attached to the staff of General Anders Viengy-Yul which was located in the Soviet Union. Thanks to that we were able to leave in 1942 for Persia and from there arrived in Israel during this vicious war.

I was only a boy when we escaped from Poland at the beginning of the war. I returned after forty-six years as the first representative of Israel in Poland at the end of a long interruption of relations and then afterwards as the first Israeli ambassador. During this time I learned very much about the part that Jews had in the development of Poland in all fields over the course of many generations, including the military – though in many cases their nationality and Judaism was not recognized because they were a minority. Now, with the establishment of the memorial, the debt which our generation owed them has been paid, thanks to your successful efforts.

The memorial is placed in the pantheon of heroism of the Israeli people, its grand design and the impressive ceremony in which some of the most important people in the nation participated, the IDF guard of honor, representatives of the government and army of Poland – all of these bear witness that your efforts were worthwhile. From my own experience I know what an effort was required of you, the difficulties you had to overcome including lobbying and negotiating and running around until you could say that you had finished. For all this, I take off my hat to you and say: Well done, well done.

Yours in friendship and admiration,
Mordecai Peltzur

Plaque to Mr. Sami Shamoon

A plaque dedicated to Mr. Sami Shamoon and Mr. Yosef Maimon and his family, the contributors to the establishment of the memorial on Mount Herzl

> To Mr. Sami Shamoon
>
> In gratitude for your generous contribution
> to the establishment of the memorial
> to the Jewish soldiers who fell in the service
> of the Polish armies during WWII
>
> **In the name of the Association of Jewish War Veterans of Polish Armies in Israel.**
>
> **Engineer Benjamin Meirchak – Chairman**
> **David Shachar – Secretary and Memorial Project Manager**

My Town –
On the Krasnosielc Community

An excerpt from The Second Generation,
a bulletin of the town of Mazovia, Poland

The Community in the Town of Krasnosielc in the Area of Northern Mazovia

The town lies about 100 kilometers northeast of Warsaw and about 25 kilometers north of Makov, approximately the same distance from Prownitz and about 50 kilometers southwest of Ostrolenka.

The entire area is called North Mazovia and had before the world war about half a million Jews. The population was usually mixed – half Poles and half Jews. There was also another minority, such as the Germans. This minority had an influence on events which happened after the start of the war.

At Krasnosielc there were 2,000 Jews. Like all the towns the community has an autonomous life and was lively. Up to World War I the main activities were religious and the importance of the town in the eyes of the townsmen was the level of learning that the governing hierarchy had: the rabbi, the *shohet*, the *hazzan* – at which yeshiva they studied and which influential family they married into. In addition, which Hasidic court they belonged to was also important. My father was a Gur Hasid and was one of the two *shohatim* in the town. He was also a *hazzan*, especially during the high holy days, and chanted from the torah on Sabbaths and holidays. He was the number two in the religious hierarchy after the rabbi. (According to the saying of our friend Mordecai Chachnover: The rabbi ended up in ghetto Makov and his fate was the fate of the blessed of Makov.)

Between the two world wars, the Haskalah, Zionism and Socialism penetrated the Jewish society of Krasnosielc and the political map was built almost as it is in Israel today.

The Bitter End of the Jews of Krasnosielc

Because of its proximity to the German border (east Prussia), the Nazi German army invaded Krasnosielc on the first day, November 3, 1939, and immediately the maltreatment of the Jewish population began. This article is too short for me to enter into detail. In short, the Polish army retreated, burned the wooden bridge over the Ulzitz River which connects Krasnosielc to the outside area. The German armored forces could not enter the town. The Germans gathered most of the males – Jews and Poles – in order to build the bridge, under the command of the German Engineering Corps. It became clear afterwards that there were disguised SS men among them who, without the knowledge of the official Army Command (the Wehrmacht), had received an order from the commander of the SS Himmler, to kill Jews at any opportunity. After a day of work they sent the Poles home and the Jews, including my father Haim Himmelfarb, blessed is his memory, were brought to the synagogue. They told the victims, "Pray to your all powerful God, perhaps He will help you," and then proceeded to shoot them. When the disgusting deed of the SS men became known to the Army Command, a squad of soldiers broke into the synagogue with a medical team, examined all the men and found that seven of them were wounded and dying. They took them to a military hospital (together with the German soldiers who were wounded in battle). They buried the dead (between 50–70 men) together with the Torah scrolls in the courtyard of the synagogue.

Some of the wounded recovered, and made it to the Russian side, where they told the terrible story of what had happened to the rest of the community.

Almost miraculously, while dealing with the details of the event and with the help of the Polish and German authorities the common grave was discovered and a memorial was set up in the courtyard of the synagogue. In the presence of a large crowd from Israel and the United States the memorial established in their memory was unveiled.

Recommendation for the President's Volunteer Citation

I hereby recommend Mr. David Shachar to receive the President's Volunteer Citation.

As a veteran Rotarian and as one who has filled the function as Governor of Rotary Israel for 1994–95 I have known David Shachar for a number of years as an enterprising activist and initiator in the movement whose whole purpose is to help one's neighbor.

Mr. David Shachar was a member of Machal in 1948, immigrated to Israel when the state was established and ever since has tied his fate to this country and its people and his way is the way of deeds and volunteering.

For example, Mr. Shachar went up to Kiryat Shmona in 1959 and lived there until 1967. During this time he was among the founders of the local Rotary Club, contributed in the field of education and placed on his record his activities for the local community.

At the same time he worked in the field of electronics, and especially in the last ten years, Mr. David Shachar began to learn and record the sources of the Jewish community in Poland, the country of his birth, the Jewish resistance during the Holocaust to the evil regime and the history of the Independence War and the revival of the Jewish people.

In these last years David has been active in establishing a memorial for the sixty Jews of his native town Krasnolsielc. This extraordinary action received appreciation and recognition on the part of government agencies in Israel and abroad.

He quickly became a walking encyclopedia in these fields. But the wide information he accumulated he did not hold to himself – he shared it with other people and lectured often on volunteering in clubs, schools and retirement homes.

With the latest wave of immigration he adopted a family of immigrants from Kiev and by this he constitutes an example of good citizenship and the symbol of beautiful Israel which absorbs immigrants with smiling faces and open arms.

In my opinion Mr. David Shachar is the volunteer par excellence, a man whose whole way is to do for the sake of the community, for the general public. I therefore feel that he constitutes a model for emulation.

Gideon Feifer

Letter from Captain Ephraim Talmon

*Despite the fact that David came to Israel only in 1948
he quickly integrated into Israeli society, and already by 1956
he earned a glowing letter of recommendation from his superior.*

Captain Ephraim Talmon, Engineer
13 Sport St. Haifa
Tel: 82671

To Whom It May Concern

I wish to confirm that Mr. David Himmelfarb was under my command beginning from May 1, 1956, as an instructor for electronic technicians.

I would like to state that he was an excellent technician with a very deep understanding of his profession. In addition, he is a dependable person with a strong work ethic.

During the entire period we worked together, I was very pleased with his performance.

(Signature)
Ephraim Talmon

Letter from the Skvirsky Family

Thank-you letter of the Skvirsky family, who immigrated to Israel from Kiev in 1990, for the Shachar family's assistance in their absorption

One of the pleasant memories of my stay in Israel is getting to know and regularly meet with the Shachar family, Chaya and David. It began in January 1990, at the ulpan for studying Hebrew. They suggested that we fill out the forms and questionnaires, and there we noted that we had no relatives in Israel, and that our friends remained in Kiev (USSR).

After a week we received a telephone call at home and in the conversation we got to know wonderful people by the name of Chaya and David Shachar. Today after some time, when we hear the words *aliya* and *Ministry of Absorption*, we remember that interesting time and think about how fortunate we were to meet such people who participated in the establishment and building of the State of Israel. For the first time we got to know the meaning of the words *Palmah, Mahal, Haganah*, etc. We heard about the War of Independence, got to know the various museums in Tel Aviv and visited Kibbutz Palmachim, took trips to the alleyways of Jaffa and went boating on the ocean to Ashdod. We spent our first holiday in Israel – Purim – at Kfar Maccabi and our first Passover seder with the Shachar family. We visited the Rothschild Park in Rishon LeZion. We went around looking for relatives but unfortunately most of them just had the same name but were not relatives.

[We experienced] unforgettable trips and evenings during the first Iraqi War. We had already begun to work – my wife, Valia, as a saleswoman in a supermarket and I as an elevator installer. Later we rented a flat on Tayassim Road (in Tel Aviv). The beginning of the absorption process we accepted calmly. We received our gas masks, we sealed our windows and doors with nylon and waited for the start of evening for the beginning of the warning sirens, in order to place the gas mask on and close the doors, etc. But when to remove the gas masks? Think we understood the instructions after eight months in Israel? After three evenings of hysteria, as missile parts fell near us, our house began to shake and we ran from the fifth floor to the cellar (the shelter) when we heard the siren go off. At the same time a lot of people left Tel Aviv. There are those who flew abroad or went south. Many would travel toward evening and would return in the morning to work, etc. Apparently David and Chaya were able to travel during this time, and despite this who but they called us up a number times in the evening in order to console us and ask if we had put on our gas masks, and to let us know when it was possible to take them off.

Thank you very much, Chaya and David. Fortunate is a country that has such people, who fulfill the meaning of its existence.

The jubilee year of the State of Israel is your jubilee year, Chaya and David, for you were the ones who worried about this country. Our grandchildren who came to Israel in 1996 spent their first Passover seder with you without understanding anything. In 1998 with you on Passover night, they already were able to read the Haggada.

Life continues and the work is important.

Thank you very much and be happy,
Skvirsky Alex, Valia, Sveta, Anna and Moshe

Impressions, Experiences and Lessons on "Operation Krasnosielc"

An article written by Nili Ben-Ari, a guide for a youth delegation from Kibbutz Tirat Tzvi, after visiting the site of the Krasnosielc murders. Among the members of the delegation was Oshra Reifen, the granddaughter of David's sister Bronia.

Several months have passed since we returned from the "trip" to Poland and we still haven't settled down. The usual definition when an Israeli goes abroad is the leave on a "tour." The trip to Poland was never a "tour." It is always a "trip" following our roots and the obscure things in our past. It is a trip that hurts and shocks, penetrating to the depths of the soul.

My trip this time came as a surprise after my first visit to Poland in 1983 during the Communist regime. I determined then that that was my personal "closing the circle" and I decided never to return again to the killing fields. One day I came across David Shachar's work in memorializing Krasnosielc and the story amazed me. My interest increased after I heard details and read the documents he discovered in German archives and the Jewish and Polish evidence of the tragic and cruel event that took place at Krasnosielc on September 5, 1939. I suddenly felt that the event was part of me.

It is important to note that the residents of all the small towns in our area had family relations and their fate was common to all of us. Since my mother came from Krasnosielc I felt that among those murdered were some of my family. I have now discovered after reading the magazine *Piatego Dnia* that among the survivors was one of my cousins who escaped with the help of a Pole. To my great sorrow he was killed later on his escape to Russia. Following my deep feelings about David Shachar's work, I wanted to be in Krasnosielc during the unveiling of the memorial on the wall of the synagogue and for the memorial in memory of those who were murdered so I decided to travel to Poland. I decided to take along my daughter Michal on the trip in order to pass on to her our roots and our origins while I was still alive. When she agreed to my proposal to accompany me, I felt obligated to add my wife to David Shachar's group, which consisted of second and third generations of survivors from Israel and the United States.

…It is difficult during this short period after the ceremony at Krasnosielc to go into and discuss the importance of this common event to all of us who came from this region. Makov, Ostrilanka, Ruzen, Tchinov, etc. Its value is great from a historical standpoint, in terms of memorializing the Jews of Poland. I believe that this is the first time documentation has been found of the military trial of the German Wehrmacht at the beginning of the war before the SS controlled the civilian population and before the attitude to Jews was determined in a formal way. The results of the trial and the documentation gave David the idea of requesting help from the present-day German authorities in financing this special project of memorializing, and also of asking for the aid and backing of the Polish authorities in similar memorializing operations in our generation and in the coming generations. In my opinion, this has no relation to our deep feelings of anger regarding anti-Semitism in general and in particular Polish anti-Semitism which has been deeply rooted for generations.

It is important for us today and for the future to do everything to remember and not forget the results of the Holocaust of our people. Still we must remember the good Christians and the importance of our behavior and relation with all peoples in order to find in them a basis of admiration for our people. The Jewish people need international backing in maintaining their existence in this area and within the Western World so that what has been done will not be repeated.

Our first worry is to ensure our future, the future of our children and coming generations. My conclusion is that every memorial project is significant both for our national memory and as a sign of the respect of other peoples. All of this does not take out of its context the importance of memorializing here in Israel, as part of the education of our children. When I turn to reconstructing for myself David Shachar's method of working I am amazed at how much one person can accomplish when he is "crazy" about the thing. I heard his story again and again about the way his work was carried out. Each time more details were added, showing new sides of the story that took many years. It was a stubborn activity without rest, although he often consulted with others. But he was the leader and doer of this great deed. I know how much blood this care has cost him – in both meanings of the expression. And as I know, not everything has yet been completed. One should value and understand the main thing: that he knew intuitively how to go step by step in investigating what happened, to gather evidence, to reach archives, in order to abstract reliable information and convince international players of the justification of his requests.

These actions led to a impressive end of the Krasnosielc affair itself.

David Shachar received recognition from the international community. At the unveiling ceremony were present representatives of the Polish authorities at all levels, representatives of the government of the region (Viboda), the mayors of the towns of Makov and Krasnosielc, representatives of the German Embassy, representatives of the Israeli Embassy, representatives of the media and others. All this was accomplished through personal public relations.

The greatness and abilities of David were expressed in the ceremony at the location of the tragic event and during his appearance before the local public and youth and before invited guests and official representatives who came to hear about the matter related to the case of Krasnosielc. David's speech in all languages was restrained and serious, and his feelings as an Israeli and a Jew in the face of this local tragedy were clear to see. He expressed also the nation's pride in our independent state and faith in a better future in relations with the Polish people. It is important to note the complicated and excellent logistic performance of David Shachar, the preparation of the memorial tablet with the names of those murdered which was made in Israel and its transportation to Poland to the intended location at Krasnosielc. All this was done with great effort, with all his spiritual and physical strength and with much money. We are all fortunate that this man of great deeds came from our people and our region. We wish to congratulate David Shachar on this great and valuable lifework which he has imparted to us and to those who will come after us.

In sum, we wish to express our gratitude to David who has realized his idea of memorializing, an idea which was with him from his early youth and which symbolized his devotion to moral projects in public life. We wish him success in his future projects.

A citation David was awarded for being a MACHAL volunteer in France 1948

ROTARY INTERNATIONAL

Service Above Self - He Profits Most Who Serves Best

KREUZSTRASSE 36, ZURICH 8, SWITZERLAND

Zurich, 13 December, 1965.

David Himelfarb, Esq.
President, The Rotary Club
Kiriat Shmona, Israel

Dear President Himelfarb:

It was indeed a great pleasure to hear from District Governor Naveh following his recent official visit to your club and to learn from him how well the Club is functioning under your devoted and energetic leadership.

He sent us a copy of your summary of club plans and objectives which amply confirms his statement concerning the intense activity of your club, and I should like to congratulate you most heartily on your work in adopting soldier-teachers in the community and on your collection of warm clothing for the needy. Most welcome, also, was the news that you have found a new meeting place in the DANZIGER school and that you will soon organize an Interact club there!

The character of your community as a new immigrants town certainly presents a special challenge to your club and it is clear that you are meeting it with resolution and effectiveness. May the good work continue!

With kindest regards and all best wishes,

Sincerely yours,

Walter Panzar
Under Secretary
lc

MINISTER OF DEFENSE

Tel-Aviv, May 11, 1988

40 Years World Machal Reunion
Machal
Tel-Aviv 69693

Dear Machal volunteers,   Mr. David Shachar, Ramat-Gan.

    It gives me great pleasure to welcome in Israel all MACHAL volunteers who came here to participate in the International Machal Convention.

    The Ministry of Defense is well aware and appreciates the personal contribution made by each one of you; there is no doubt that this contribution as well as the personal sacrifices were all part of the great endeavour made at the time to build the new State of Israel and the Israel Defense Forces, and you should all be proud of the role you played towards achieving this goal.

    I sincerely hope that you will enjoy the reunion intended to mark the fortieth anniversary of the State of Israel.

With best wishes,

                                              Yours sincerely,

                                              Y. Rabin
                                         Minister of Defense

ראש הממשלה
Prime Minister

November 11, 1999
ב' כסלו, תש"ס

Dear David,

On the occasion of the establishing of a monument in memory of the Jewish soldiers who gave their lives while serving in the Polish Army, I commend you and all those involved in preserving the names of the fallen, in that cursed war.

The recognition awarded to you today by the Government of Poland, for your contribution and involvement in perpetuating the fallen, is but a minor part in the chapter of life which is the basis of our existence in the State of Israel.

With pride, I salute you today.

Sincerely yours,

E. Barak

Ehud Barak

Mr. David Shahar
Rehov Uziel 116
Ramat Gan

cc: H.E. Ambassador Maciej Kozlowski, Republic of Poland

Jerusalem, Israel

EMBASSY
OF THE REPUBLIC OF POLAND
IN ISRAEL
AMBASSADOR

Tel-Aviv, February 14, 2001.

His Excellency
Mr. Moshe Katsav
President of the State of Israel
Jerusalem

Dear Mr. President,

I have the honour to inform you that I personally know Mr. David Shachar since I started my mission in Israel in the summer of 1999. Mr. David Shachar has acted with distinction in order to broaden and further develop good relations between Poland and Israel, advantageous to both our countries.

The initiatives undertaken by Mr. David Shachar, among others the constructions of a Monument to commemorate the Jewish Soldiers of Polish Armies at Mount Herzel in Jerusalem and the mounting of a Plaque to commemorate the Jewish victims of Nazi atrocities in Krasnosielec, Poland, will be remembered as contributing to the spirit of traditional friendship of our two nations, for the benefit of peace and international understanding.

Please accept, dear Mr. President, the assurances of my highest consideration.

Maciej Kozłowski

Translation

PRESERVATION BOARD
OF
RESISTANCE &TORTURE MEMORIALS

Andrzey PRZEWOZNIK, Secretary

November 6, 2003

To: David Shachar
Israel

Dear Sir,

We are pleased to inform you that, in accordance with your request,

the monuments as well as the plaque dedicated to the murdered

Polish citizens of Jewish nationality in Krasnosielc on September 5, 1939,

have been added to the Central Memorial Registry of National Local Evidences.

Respectfully yours,